MESSY, MOODY, MAGIC

BY

ANSHIKA SINGH

ISBN: 978-93-5469-871-2

First Edition, January 2026

Printed in India

About the Author

Anshika Singh is a young writer who believes in capturing emotions as they are—messy, honest, and deeply human. Messy, Moody, Magic is her first book, written straight from the heart and inspired by the everyday moments most people overlook. She hopes her words bring comfort, clarity, and connection to anyone who reads them.

Writing this book felt like opening my diary to the world—raw, real, and sometimes terrifying. But I never walked this path alone.

To my parents, Mr. Deep Ranjan Singh and Mrs. Simple Singh, thank you for being the quiet strength behind every chapter. Your patience, unconditional love, and belief in me gave me the courage to write even when I doubted myself. This book is, in many ways, a reflection of the resilience and values you've given me.

To Mr. Nitin, thank you for giving this book a face that speaks before the words do.

To everyone who inspired this book—whether through a message, a shared story, or simply your presence in my life—this is for you. I see your mess. I feel your moods. And I believe in your magic.

To the books and authors that carried me through my own growing up, thank you for reminding me how words can heal.

And finally, to the younger version of me—you needed this book, and I hope I've done you justice, to anyone who has ever cried in a bathroom stall, overthought every text, felt too much, loved too deeply, or still showed up every day—messy, moody, and magical—this one's for you.
With all my love and gratitude,
Anshika Singh

Hey you,

Welcome to Messy, Moody, Magic — a no-filter, no-judgment space for anyone trying to make sense of their world. I wrote this because I've been there too — confused, overwhelmed, and constantly wondering if I'm enough. Sound familiar?

From confidence to comparison, friendships to breakdowns, this book dives into the real stuff — the awkward, emotional, unpredictable chaos that comes with simply being human. I've woven in life lessons, honest reflections, and inspiration drawn from both the best days and the hardest ones.

This isn't about being perfect. It's about embracing the mess, understanding yourself a little better, and finding the magic anyway.

Let's go

Dedication

To everyone who ever felt like

the main character of their own chaos—

This book is for you.

And to the younger me,

who didn't know she'd make it this far

TABLE OF CONTENTS

Introduction

There are days when life feels like a puzzle, I was never given the full picture of. Days when I wake up confident, ready to take on the world… and by evening, I'm questioning everything about myself. Maybe you've felt that too — the slow rise of doubt, the sudden rush of emotion, the confusion of being both strong and sensitive at the same time.

Messy, Moody, Magic was born somewhere between those extremes.

I didn't write this book from a mountaintop of wisdom. I wrote it from the floor, from my bed, from late-night thoughts and early-morning clarity. I wrote it while figuring myself out, losing myself a little, and becoming myself again. These pages are not instructions; they are reflections. Not lessons, but reminders. Not answers, but honest moments.

This book is my attempt to make sense of the chaos inside me — the kind that makes you feel too much, dream too much, care too much, break too much, but also the kind that makes you powerful in ways you don't always notice.

You'll find a lot here:

• Thoughts I never said out loud

- Emotions, I didn't know how to explain
- Questions I was too scared to ask
- Moments I thought were just mine — but maybe aren't
- Tiny sparks of magic I found in the middle of my messy days

If you're the kind of person whose heart gets heavy for no reason, whose mood shifts like sunlight through clouds, who loves deeply and hurts quietly — then I think you'll feel at home in this book.

You don't need to be "fixed" to be worthy. You don't need to be perfectly composed to be lovable. You don't need to have everything figured out to be magical. You just need to be real honest human.

That's enough. It has always been enough.

So, as you read, I hope you don't just see my story — you see your own reflections gently peeking through the words. I hope something here touches you, comforts you, or simply makes you feel understood in a world that often forgets softness exists.

Welcome to this space. Welcome to the mess, the moods, and the magic.

Let's begin.

Chapter 1

Who Even Am I?

Let's be honest—figuring out who you *really* are feels a lot like trying to solve a jigsaw puzzle in the dark... without the box cover. And half the pieces are missing. And someone keeps switching out the pieces when you're not looking. One minute, you're vibing hard with Taylor Swift's *Mirrorball* on repeat, twirling around your room like you're the star of a heartbreak movie... and the next? You're staring at your ceiling at 2 a.m., wondering if you're even remotely interesting or just another background character in everyone else's life.

Some days, you're totally that mysterious main character who journals in a café, listens to indie playlists, and has their whole aesthetic *together.* And then there are days when you're in your oversized hoodie, eating cereal out of a mug, and trying not to cry over a Chemistry worksheet you *definitely* don't understand. Sound familiar?

Here's the truth no one puts on Instagram: figuring yourself out is messy. It's not a straight road, it's not a checklist, and it's definitely not something you just "know." It's more like wandering through a huge thrift store—you're picking up random things that seem *so you* in the moment: vintage sunglasses, a sparkly diary, a weird mug shaped like a frog. And then later, you're like... why did I even think this was my vibe?

One week, you're convinced you're going to be a neurosurgeon and start watching intense medical documentaries like you're preparing for an exam. The next week, you're designing tote bags on Canva, binge-watching TED Talks about entrepreneurship, and planning your million-dollar skincare brand with your best friend. You go from watching legal drama series and saying "Objection, Your Honor" out loud, to Googling "how to become a travel vlogger" because a random YouTube video made it look like a dream life. It's exhausting, hilarious, and weirdly beautiful.

And then comes *that* question. You know the one.

"So, what do you want to be when you grow up?"

Ma'am. Sir. Uncle. Auntie. I don't even know what I want for dinner tonight, please. Like, how am I supposed to figure out my *entire life path* when I can barely commit to a favorite cereal or stick to a single Pinterest board aesthetic for more than two weeks?

But here's the good news—no one actually has it all figured out. Not your friend who swears they're going to be a tech genius. Not your cousin who posts "grind never stops" selfies every other day. Not even the adults are asking you these questions. (Plot twist: most of them are still figuring it out, too.)

You are allowed to try things on for size. You're allowed to change your mind. You're allowed to be a little lost, a little curious, and a whole lot chaotic.

Because of this "figuring it out" phase? It's where all the magic happens.

You learn by exploring, by making cringey mistakes, by being obsessed with random things, by failing, by pivoting, by feeling deeply, and by laughing at how confusing it all is. Your identity isn't a fixed label—it's a living, breathing, evolving story. And *you* get to be the author. So next time someone asks you who you are or what you want to be, don't panic. Just smile and say,

"Right now, I'm a work-in-progress—and that's actually kind of exciting."

Identity Crisis 101: You Are Not Broken

Let's get one thing straight: if you've ever stared into your bathroom mirror and thought, *"Who even am I?"*—congratulations, you're officially human.

Most teens go through an identity crisis. Actually—scratch that—most *humans* do. Multiple times. It's like a rite of passage that no one really talks about until you're already halfway into an emotional spiral, googling "how to find your purpose" at 1:36 a.m. with lo-fi beats playing in the background.

But because you're young, everyone assumes you should just "figure it out" like it's a timed quiz. As if one morning

you'll wake up, stretch, and suddenly know your passions, life goals, fashion aesthetic, and whether you're an introvert or just socially exhausted. *(Spoiler: even adults don't have all this sorted.)*

You're expected to be confident—but not arrogant.

Ambitious—but not intimidating.

Pretty—but not too aware of it.

Emotional—butnot "dramatic."

Smart—but definitely not the kind of smart that corrects someone in class (because ew, nerd).

So basically... you're supposed to be a unicorn.

But like, a humble unicorn who doesn't take up too much space.

Umm, what?

Let's call it what it is: *an impossible manual* written by society that makes zero sense. And here you are, trying to build a whole personality while walking that tightrope of being "just enough" for everyone. It's exhausting.

Now, here's the part no one says enough—

You are not broken. You're becoming.

Your identity isn't some final version you magically unlock at age 17. It's more like a playlist—you add some songs, remove a few, go through a country music phase you don't talk about, and slowly discover what feels *true* to *you*. Your taste will change. Your voice will evolve. Your beliefs will shift. And that's not failure—that's *growth.*

One year, you might be all about boho skirts and bookish vibes, and the next, you're rocking graphic tees and watching crime documentaries like you're prepping to join the FBI. One month, you're obsessed with being "that girl" who wakes up at 5 a.m., drinks green juice, and journals. And next month? You're bingeing rom-coms in bed and surviving solely on iced coffee and vibes. And it's okay. You're allowed to explore and pivot and unlearn and change your mind.

You're not falling behind—you're just *collecting pieces* of yourself. You're a Pinterest board in real life. You're a mood swing and a masterpiece. You're a draft that's being revised in real time.

Some of the confusion you feel? That's freedom in disguise.

Some of the chaos in your brain? That's just your soul trying on different outfits.

You don't need to have a brand. Or an aesthetic. Or a 10-year plan. You just need to stay curious and compassionate—with yourself, especially. So next time you feel like you're too much or not enough, just remember: you're *in progress.* And that's exactly where you're supposed to be. Some of the mess is *growth*. Some of the uncertainty is *freedom.*

Story Time: Many Versions of Me

Let me take you back to 11th grade. Ah, yes, the era of bad decisions, hormonal mood swings, and believing one Instagram story could ruin your entire reputation. At that time, I was basically starring in my own multi-character sitcom.

Why? Because I had not one, not two, but three friend circles.

Circle One:

The Overachievers – They had color-coded notes, bullet journals, and a 5-year plan. They genuinely enjoyed group projects. I sat with them in class pretending I, too, found macroeconomics thrilling. I spoke only when spoken to. My handwriting? Immaculate. My personality? On aeroplane mode.

Circle Two:

The Meme Lords – This squad was absolute chaos. Group chats are popping off 24/7 with cursed memes, voice notes that made zero sense, and inside jokes that could never be explained to outsiders without sounding like actual lunatics. With them, I was sarcastic, loud, and borderline unhinged. I communicated mostly in TikTok audios and SpongeBob references.

Circle Three:

The Eyeliner Pros – These were the effortlessly cool kids. The kind who wore leather jackets in 40-degree heat and somehow never sweat. Their eyeliner? Razor sharp. Their music taste? Underground. Their selfies? Olympic-level. With them, I tried so hard to be chill. I said things like, "Yeah, I don't really care about marks", right after crying over a B+. I laughed like I was in a Netflix show. I used words like "vibe check" even when no one asked.

And here's the problem: with each group, I shape-shifted. Like, a chameleon in a thrift store. In one group, I was the smart, soft-spoken "not like other girls" type. In another, I was the class clown. And in the last one, I was mysterious and edgy (in my mind at least).

Eventually, I was like... okay, but **who even am I**?

Because at some point, I started losing track. Like I'd walk into the classroom and have to mentally download which version of me I needed to be that day.

Then came *The Moment.*

One random Tuesday evening, after pretending to be cool all day (and failing—my eyeliner smudged and I tripped over my own shoelace in front of my crush), I flopped on my bed, stared at the ceiling fan, and thought:

"If I disappeared right now..., would I even miss myself?"

Existential crisis unlocked. Level 10 activated. So naturally, I did the most *dramatic teenage thing* ever. I lit a candle. (A cinnamon-scented one, obviously.) Opened a dusty notebook. And wrote like I was the main character in a sad indie film. I made a list. Not for marks. Not for clout. Not to impress anyone.

Just a list of things I genuinely loved when no one was watching:

Baking cupcakes in a messy kitchen with bad 2010s music blasting

Watching Studio Ghibli movies on loop like they were therapy

Writing poetry, I never posted (because cringe, obviously)

Talking to plants. Yes, *talking*. They're better listeners than most humans.

And reading that chaotic, wholesome, slightly embarrassing list? It hit me like a truth bomb. The real me wasn't cool, or curated, or "aesthetic." She was awkward. Soft. A little weird. Messy but magical. Goofy but deep. Curious and dramatic and *real*. And that? That was enough. Not for the group chats. Not for the fake chill selfies.

-But for me.

Real Talk: You're Allowed to Change

Hey. Come closer. I've got a secret for you—one that no one really says out loud, but you need to hear:

You are allowed to change.

Yup. That's it. No guilt, no apology, no over-explaining required. You're allowed to wake up one day and realize you no longer vibe with that show you used to binge.

You're allowed to drift away from a friendship that once felt like everything but now just feels... forced. You're allowed to drop a hobby you thought you'd love forever. You're even allowed to look in the mirror and think, *"Wait... I don't really know who I am right now."*

That's not failure.

That's not being fake.

That's *evolution.*

Some days, you'll feel powerful—like you could take over the world with a messy bun and a to-do list. Other days, you'll feel like a soggy tissue on the floor of an emotionally unstable teenager's bedroom. *(Still valid. Still lovable.)*

And that's a rollercoaster? That doesn't mean you're broken. It means you're *human.* There's a weird pressure to "always know who you are," as if your identity is a fixed Instagram bio that you can't edit. But real life isn't like that. You're not a final draft. You're a living, breathing *work-in-progress*—and that's a beautiful thing. So takes a deep breath. Let go of the guilt. Unclench your shoulders.

You don't have to have it all figured out right now. You're **not** running late. You're not falling behind. You're just growing.

And while we're being real, let's get this straight:

You are **not** your:

- GPA or grades
- Follower count or likes
- Family's expectations
- Crush's attention or lack of it

You are so much more.

You're the songs you hum when no one's around. You're the way your eyes light up when you talk about something you love. You're the weird little ideas in your Notes app. You're a plot twist waiting to happen. You're soft and strong and silly and scared and *trying*, and that's already enough. You don't need to "pick a lane" or "decide who you are" at 15 or 19 or even 25. Life will give you many versions of yourself—and the best thing you can do is meet them with kindness. So next time you feel like you've changed too much or you're losing your sense of self, I want you to remember this.

"It's not the end. It's just the next chapter. And you, my love, are the author"

Now go give yourself a little grace. Maybe even a snack. You're doing better than you think.

Wisdom Drop

In The Gifts of Imperfection, Brené Brown says:

"Authenticity is the daily practice of letting go of who we think we're supposed to be and embracing who we are."

"It's not about finding yourself. It's about returning to yourself. Every. Single. Day."

Chapter 2

You're Not "Too Much" — They're Just Not Enough

"You're not too loud. Too sensitive. Too intense. You're just not for people who dim your shine to feel better about their own."

- The Fear of Being "Too Much"

Let's talk about *that* feeling—the one that creeps in after someone calls you "extra," rolls their eyes when you get excited, or tells you to "calm down" when your emotions get a little loud.

Have you ever been told things like:

- "Why are you so emotional all the time?"
- "You overthink everything."
- "You're too dramatic, just chill."

It stings, doesn't it?

Even if they say it like a joke... it sinks in.

Little by little, you start to wonder if maybe you are too much. Too loud. Too soft. Too intense. Too sensitive. Too *everything.*

So, what do you do?

You shrink.

You quiet your voice. You laugh a little less loudly. You edit your texts five times before sending them. You rehearse your opinions in your head to make sure they're "palatable." You stop crying in front of people, even when your heart's breaking. Because somewhere along the way, *you* were taught that being fully you was something to apologize for. But here's a little truth bomb—and I want you to hear this like I'm saying it while holding your hand:

You were never "too much."

You were just around people who were too little to hold space for your fullness.

Your emotions? Aren't too much. They're *deep.*

Your enthusiasm? It isn't embarrassing. It's *beautiful.*

Are you overthinking? It isn't annoying. It's a sign that you *care.*

Your "drama"? Maybe it's not drama at all. Maybe it's just passion with a little glitter. The problem was never you. The problem is a world that keeps trying to cram us into tidy little boxes labeled "acceptable," "easy to digest," "quiet," "cute," "normal."

But you?

You were made for more. You were made to feel deeply. To take up space. To ask too many questions. To love too loudly. To cry when things hurt. To laugh until you snort. To care so fiercely it scares people. And sure, not everyone will get you. Not everyone is meant to.

But your people—the ones who see you?

They'll never ask you to tone it down. They'll say, "I love how much you feel. It makes me feel safe to feel too." So please, stop editing yourself to fit into someone else's idea of "enough." You are already enough. And *then some.*

Let the world adjust to you. The problem isn't you. The problem is that the world is trying to fit you into boxes you were never meant to fit into.

Story time: A Little Story from My Life

Let me take you back to 9th grade—a time of group chats, terrible cafeteria snacks, and trying way too hard to fit into friend circles that made me feel like a walking *cringe compilation.*

There was this group I hung out with. On the surface, we were "friends." We ate lunch together, tagged each other in memes, took selfies with the dog filter... You know, *peak bestie behavior*. But underneath? It felt like I was always walking on emotional eggshells. Anytime I showed real feelings—*I mean, real ones*—they made me feel like I was doing something wrong. If I cried, even a little, it was:

"Ugh, why are you so sensitive all the time?"

If I got excited about something—like discovering a new moon phase in astrology or geeking out over an anime character—they'd roll their eyes and go:

"You're being so extra."

When I read one of my poems out loud in English class (which took, like, all the courage I had), one of them whispered, "Why is she always so *deep* about everything?" It didn't seem like a big deal at first. But slowly, quietly, I started shrinking.

I started second-guessing every sentence before I spoke. I smiled, but only politely. I laughed, but not the real, belly-shaking kind that used to make my cheeks hurt. I stopped bringing up the things I loved. I stopped showing up as *me.*

And the worst part?

I thought they were *right*. I thought maybe I was too much. Then came the plot twist.

It was one of those random Tuesdays when nothing big was supposed to happen. I got switched to a new art class mid-term (thanks to a timetable mess-up), and I ended up sitting next to this girl I'd never talked to before. She had blue eyeliner and paint on her hoodie and the most *genuine energy* I'd felt in a long time.

I was sketching something silly on the corner of my paper—some stars and a line of poetry I'd randomly thought of—and she leaned over and said,

"Whoa. That's actually so cool. I love how passionate you are. It's refreshing."

Refreshing.

That word cracked something open in me. It felt like the first time someone saw me—not just tolerated me. And in that tiny moment, something clicked.

Maybe I wasn't "too much."

Maybe I wasn't dramatic or annoying or overly emotional.

Maybe I was just too *magical* for people who didn't know how to appreciate depth, wonder, or big, beautiful feelings.

After that day, I didn't magically un-shrink. I still had moments where I zipped myself up to be more "digestible." But I started to notice the difference. Some people will ask you to dim your light. And then, some people will hand you a mirror and say,

"Look how bright you shine."

Now, I protect my sparkle.

Now, I choose people who don't just *allow* me to be fully me, but *celebrate* it. So, if you've ever been made to feel like you're "too much," I just want to say:

No, love. You're just not meant to be watered down.

The Life Lesson

Here's something I learned the hard way, and maybe you have too:

People who are uncomfortable with your fire will always try to put it out.

They'll say you're "too intense."

They'll call your ambition "arrogance."

They'll label your kindness as "clingy," your vulnerability as "attention-seeking," and your confidence as "too much."

But here's the thing—**your fire isn't the problem.**

Some people just prefer things dim. It's not your job to set yourself on fire just to keep someone else warm. It's also not your job to extinguish your glow just because someone else refuses to wear sunglasses.

The *right* people?

The ones meant for you?

They'll do something beautiful. They'll pull up a chair beside your fire... and warm their hands by it. They'll see the way your eyes light up when you talk about something you love, and they won't make fun of it. They'll notice when your voice trembles with emotion, and they won't call you dramatic—they'll lean in and say, "Tell me more." They'll hear your dreams and instead of telling you to be "realistic," they'll say, "How can I help?"

But here's the catch. Before you find those people, you'll probably meet a few who misunderstand you. Maybe more than a few. People who raise an eyebrow when you cry over something small—because they've never learned how to feel deeply. People who roll their eyes when you speak up—because your voice reminds them of their own silence. People who laugh when you dream big—because they gave up on there a long time ago.

And you? You'll be tempted to shrink.

You'll wonder, *"Am I really that hard to love?"*

You'll try being quieter, softer, smaller—more "manageable."

But here's your life lesson, right here, right now:

Don't ever shrink to make others feel safe.

You are not here to be comfortable. You are not here to fit neatly into a box labeled "normal." You are not here to make yourself less sparkly, less soulful, less you. You're not meant to be safe. You're meant to be *authentically you.* Big-hearted. Loud-laughing. Tear-shedding. Messy and magical and unapologetically alive. So, protect your fire. Nurture it. Let it dance wildly. And trust that the right people—the ones who are meant to walk this path with you—will never fear your flame. They'll sit beside you. Smile. And say,

"Wow. It's so warm here."

Reminder, You Need

You're not here to make yourself palatable to people who were never even hungry for your kind of magic.

Let that sink in for a second.

You were never meant to be bite-sized. You were never meant to be carefully packaged, watered down, or easy to swallow.

You were made to be *flavorful.* To be felt. To be remembered.

And yet, here you are—maybe slowly silencing yourself in conversations, maybe making your laugh quieter, maybe editing the way you express joy or speak your truth... just to be more "likeable." More "normal." More *digestible.*

Why? Because someone once said you were too much. Because you were told to take it down a notch. Because someone smirked when you shared something that mattered to you.

So, you shrank a little. And then a little more. Until parts of you started to feel like a "problem" you needed to fix.

But let's get real for a second.

If This Sounds Like You...

• You’ve been told you’re too talkative, like your thoughts are supposed to come with a mute button.
• You’ve been teased for caring too deeply—as if empathy was something to be embarrassed about.
• You’ve been made to feel like your energy is too loud, too much, too everything.

Here’s your truth bomb:

“Your light is not a burden. It’s a gift”

Read that again. Slower this time.

You weren’t meant to blend in. You weren’t meant to fit someone else’s idea of “just right.” You were made to glow exactly as you are—unfiltered, uncensored, unbothered. There is *nothing wrong* with feeling things fully. There is *nothing wrong* with having big ideas and bigger dreams. There is *nothing wrong* with showing up as your full, beautiful, chaotic self. You don’t need to ask for permission to be the real you. You don’t need to apologize for the space you take up. You don’t need to tone it down for people who were never tuned in to begin with.

So, repeat after me:

I will not apologies for being all that I am.

My voice matters.

My energy is sacred.

My light is not too much.

My light is a gift.

And anyone who can't handle that?

They're simply not ready for your kind of magic. Let them scroll past. Let them misunderstand. Let them go. Because your people—the real ones?

They'll see your light and say,

"Finally. There you are."

What You Can Try Right now :

• Text a friend who *gets you* and thank them.
• Journal what "being too much" really means to you — is it really bad, or is it powerful?
• Next time someone calls you "too emotional," ask yourself: *Would I want to be less of myself to please them?* (Spoiler: No. A Message to the Real Ones:

"You're not extra. You're extraordinary."

Chapter 3

Friendship Red Flags

Because real friends don't drain your soul.

The Chaos We Call Friendship

Friendship during your teen years?

It's like being dropped in the middle of a chaotic group project—no instructions, no exit strategy, and someone *always* has drama. One second, you're giggling over inside jokes, eating fries off each other's plates, and planning matching outfits...

And the next?

You're left on read.

You're hearing your secrets from someone else's mouth.

You're suddenly "too much," or worse—**not enough**.

Let's be honest: Teen friendships are intense. Like, main-character-movie-montage intense. They can make you feel high on life... or completely crushed in seconds.

But here's the *plot twist* they never warned you about:

Not every friendship is forever. And not every friend is good for your soul. Not all friendships are meant to last—and not all friends are good for your peace of mind.

We were raised on fairy tales and high school movies that sold us the dream of a "BFF for life."

The matching bracelets . The sleepovers. The reels and loyalty pacts sealed with Pringles and Pinky promises .But no one taught us how to recognize the quiet chaos:

- The friend who only texts when they need something.
- The one who subtly competes with you.
- The "joking" insults that actually sting.
- The group that turns silent when you walk in.
- The constant pressure to keep up, fit in, and not speak up when something feels... off.

Let's call it what it is:

Toxic friendships are real—and they hurt. Sometimes more than breakups.

And you?

You deserve better. You deserve friendships that feel like safety, not survival.

You deserve friends who clap when you win, check in when you're quiet, and stick around without making you feel like you're walking on eggshells.

So, let's rewrite the script.

Let's talk about how to spot the red flags, how to stand your ground, and how to build friendships that feel like sunlight—not storm clouds.

Ready?

Let's go friend-hunting—with eyes wide open this time.

A True Story: When My "Bestie" Became a Stranger

I had one best friend. Let's call her Aanya.

We met in 7th grade, clicked instantly, and soon we were inseparable—matching notebooks, inside jokes, 100-picture selfie dumps, all of it. Everyone thought we were "friendship goals," and maybe I believed it, too. But slowly, I started feeling like a side character in my own story.

Aanya had this charm that pulled people in. She was funny, loud, confident—and I admired her. But it began to feel like admiration turned into intimidation.

She'd **mock my style**, but frame it as a "joke."

She'd **copy my project ideas** and present them as her own.

She'd **vanish for days,** only to come back when she needed help.

Once, I got a lead role in our school play—and instead of being excited for me, she said, *"They probably just needed someone last-minute."* I laughed it off. Again.

But the moment that shattered everything?

I had shared something really personal with her—about my anxiety. One day during lunch, in front of a group, she blurted out, "Don't mind her. You know how she gets, *with her little panic attacks and all."*

Everyone laughed. My heart didn't. I went home that day feeling exposed, betrayed, and stupid for trusting her.

Ending the friendship wasn't a grand, dramatic scene. There was no final fight, no closure speech.

I just stopped trying. I stopped explaining myself, stopped texting first, stopped showing up.

And you know what happened?

Nothing.

She didn't even notice. And that's when I realized—I had been watering a plant that wasn't even real. It hurt. But healing hurt less than holding on.

Now, years later, I'm surrounded by people who cheer for me loudly, who sit with me silently when I'm low, who celebrate my weirdness instead of mocking it. That's what real friendship looks like.

Friendship Red Flags (a.k.a. When to Rethink the Group Chat)

So, you're vibing with a friend group or a certain someone, but deep down, something feels... off. Maybe it's the weird tension. Maybe it's how drained you feel after hanging out. Maybe it's just that little voice in your head saying, *"This isn't it."*

Let's decode that gut feeling. Here are some friendship red flags that deserve a closer look:

1. You're Always the Punchline.

It's one thing to tease your bestie about their snack obsession. It's another thing to constantly be made fun of in a way that makes you feel small. If every "joke" is at your expense—and it's never funny to you—it's not humor. It's hurt.

2. They Compete Instead of Celebrate.

You tell them you got an A, and they change the subject. You post a glow-up pic, and they don't even throw you a "fire". If your wins feel like threats to them, that's a them-problem—not a you-problem.

3. They Talk About Others... and Probably About You.

It feels kind of thrilling when someone spills the tea—until you realize your own business might be next. If they gossip *with* you, chances are they gossip *about* you too.

4. It's Always on You to Fix Things.

They ghost you, flake on plans, snap at you—and somehow, *you* end up apologizing, or feeling guilty. Friendship isn't supposed to be emotional gymnastics.

5. You Feel Drained After Hanging Out.

This is a big one. The people you spend time with should *energize* you, not exhaust you.

If you're constantly anxious, left out, or walking on eggshells, that's your sign, bestie.

When the Group Chat Feels Like a Battle Zone: Healing from a Friendship Breakup

Let's be real. Losing a friend can hit harder than a breakup. No one really prepares you for that ache—the empty seat at lunch, the missing "wyd?" text, the old photos that now feel like a lie. But here's what you *need* to hear:

1. It's Okay to Grieve.
Crying? Valid.
Missing them even though they hurt you?
Normal. Friendship breakups *hurt* because they matter. Give yourself space to feel it all.

2. You Don't Need Closure to Move On.
Not every friendship ends with a heart-to-heart or a dramatic "we need to talk."
Sometimes, people just change. Or they were never who you thought they were. And that's still closure.

3. Block. Mute. Distance.
Protect your peace. You don't need to keep watching their stories or decoding their shady captions.

It's not petty—it's self-respect.

4. Find Your People—The Real Ones.
There *are* friends out there who will love you loudly, protect you fiercely, and show up even on your worst days. You don't have to chase them. You just have to be *you.*
The right people will stay.

Real Talk Reminder:

Outgrowing friendships doesn't make you a bad person.
Setting boundaries doesn't mean you're "too sensitive."
Choosing peace over drama? That's growth.

How to Build Healthy Friendships (That Don't Feel Like a Full-Time Job)

Okay, now that we've dodged the drama and deleted the emotional vampires from our contacts...

Let's talk about what *real* friendship should feel like. Spoiler: It's not *draining*, it's *nourishing*. Healthy friendships are like soft hoodies and playlists that just get you comfortable, warm, and safe.

So how do you find *those* kinds of connections?

1. Start With You.
Before anything else: *Are you being the kind of friend you want to attract?*

Kindness, honesty, accountability—it all starts with you. Treat others with genuine care, but don't shrink or fake it just to fit in. Your authenticity is your people-magnet.

2. Look for Consistency, Not Intensity.
A real friend isn't just the one who hypes you up at parties—it's the one who checks in after. They show up when it's boring, messy, or inconvenient.
Hot take: Loyalty is quiet. And rare. Keep those people close.

3. Notice How You Feel Around Them.
You should feel safe being your weird, magical, unfiltered self. If you leave hangouts feeling more YOU—not less—that's your green flag.

4. Respect Goes Both Ways.
Healthy friends:

- Apologies when they mess up.
- Listen when you talk.
- Don't joke about your insecurities.

And guess what? You do the same back. Mutual respect = friendship that lasts.

5. It's Okay to Have Different Friends for Different Things.

Not every friend needs to be your soulmate. Some friends are for late-night rants. Some are for memes and matcha runs. Some are your emotional support humans. And some fade with time—and that's okay, too.

Gen-Z Quote Break

"Real friends feel like home, not homework."

Chapter 4

Social Media ≠ Self-Worth

"Filters may blur your freckles, but they shouldn't blur your reality."

The Scroll Trap, *aka how 5 minutes on your phone can ruin your entire vibe.*

It always starts off so chill.

You pick up your phone just to "reply to one message." Maybe you tell yourself you'll scroll for *five minutes tops* — just a quick brain break. No harm done, right?

But thirty minutes later, you're not texting anymore. You're knee-deep in a rabbit hole of back-to-back reels. One second, you're laughing at a cat wearing sunglasses, and the next, you're watching some girl clean her aesthetic room that looks straight out of a Pinterest board, while your own floor is hidden under a pile of mismatched socks and half-finished homework.

Then come the skincare routines. The "glow-up" transformations. The couples dancing to choreographed songs in color-coordinated pyjamas. And suddenly, without realizing it, your brain whispers something cruel:

"Why doesn't my life look like that?"

"Why don't I look like that?"

I've been there — more times than I'd like to admit. I remember one particular night. I was lying in bed, wrapped in my blanket like a burrito, hair in a bun that was definitely 48 hours past cute. I started scrolling through this girl's Insta profile — you know the type. Every post looked like a magazine shoot. She was always glowing, always somewhere dreamy, with latte art and sunset selfies and captions like "just vibing...".

I didn't even realize it, but my face dropped. I found myself zooming in on my own selfies, suddenly noticing all the "flaws" I hadn't seen before. I ended up deleting three pictures from my profile. Just like that. Not because they were bad... but because they weren't *her.*

And then I went to bed — not inspired, not entertained — just feeling... less.

But here's the plot twist no one talks about:

That girl? She's not perfect either.

She has bad days, too. Days when she cries on the bathroom floor. Fights with her parents. Anxiety, she doesn't post about. Awkward moments, bad selfies, bloated mornings. And chances are, she's looked at someone else's profile and felt "not enough" too.

We're all stuck in the same scroll trap. Social media isn't *real life*. It's the highlight reel. It's the best angles with 10 tries and 3 filters. It's the one day out of 30 when someone feels confident enough to post.

And yet, here we are — comparing our behind-the-scenes chaos to someone else's staged moment.

It's like watching the final cut of a movie and feeling bad because your *blooper reel* doesn't match.

Here's your reminder:

Your mess, your breakouts, your off-days, your unfiltered moments — they are real. They are human. They are *magic*.

You don't need to glow like someone else to shine in your own way.

So, the next time the scroll trap comes for you, take a breath.

Put the phone down.

Look around.

You are more than enough, *offline*.

The Illusion of "Perfect"

How one scroll can make you question your entire life.

Okay, confession time.

Have you ever felt jealous of someone's feed even though you know it's curated? Have you ever been chilling in your bed — like full-on cosy gremlin mode, hoodie on, crumbs on your blanket — and you decide to just "check Insta really quick"?

You open the app and boom.

Your screen lights up with someone's perfect golden-hour selfie, captioned "just a normal day" with 500 fire emojis in the comments.

You see her smooth skin, her soft smile, the glittery background, her entire vibe looking like she walked out of a Pinterest board... and suddenly, you're questioning everything.

"Wait... why doesn't my face glow like that?"

"Why is my life not that aesthetic?"

"Am I doing something wrong?"

Even though you know—like *actually know*—that it's all curated.

You know there's probably a filter. You *know* that angle took 40 tries.

And yet, your brain hits you with a sucker punch of self-doubt anyway.

I call this: social distortion.

It's like social comparison... but on steroids.

You see someone post a party video with glitter balloons, coordinated outfits, fairy lights, and group hugs. Suddenly, your wholesome night in with instant noodles and a rewatch of "The Summer I Turned Pretty" feels *lame.*

Their fun becomes your FOMO. Their filter becomes your flaw. Their performance becomes your personal standard. But let's zoom out. You didn't see the meltdown she had while doing her eyeliner. You didn't see the moments they argued over who wasn't invited. You didn't see the girl who forced herself to smile through the anxiety just to "look okay" in the boomerang. You didn't see the 45 rejected photos on her camera roll before she posted that one.

Social media is not real life.

It's the highlight reel with the bloopers deleted.

It's like everyone is putting on a show — a shiny, pastel-filtered performance — and we're sitting in the audience thinking we're the only ones who feel out of place.

But newsflash: even the people who seem "perfect"?

They feel it too. They also scroll and compare. They also look at someone else and feel like they're not enough. And don't even get me started on the numbers. How many likes did I get? Did they comment? Did I hit 1K followers yet?

Suddenly, your worth feels glued to a screen.

And it's wild how ten little hearts can make you feel good about yourself... or crush your confidence in seconds.

But let me say this loud for the people in the back:

You are not your likes. You are not your followers. You are not your engagement rate.

You are not a brand. You're a **person**. A person who sings off-key in the shower. A person who has rough skin days and anxiety spirals, and weird dancing skills. A person who might not have the "perfect feed" — but has real friends, real feelings, and real growth happening behind the scenes.

And you know what?

That is way cooler than anything a filter can fake.

So next time you're scrolling and suddenly feel like your life doesn't measure up, try this:

Pause.

Put the phone down.

Breathe.

And remind yourself:

That girl with the perfect mirror selfie?

She's human too.

She has bloated days. She has insecurities. She cries sometimes.

Just like you. Just like all of us.

The illusion of "perfect" is powerful.

But you?

You're even more powerful when you stop chasing it and start loving your real, raw, wonderful self — exactly as you are.

We tend to measure our worth in likes, comments, and follower counts. But numbers don't define you. They never did.

What You Don't See

• You don't see the 50 pictures taken before that one perfect post.
• You don't see the Face tune edits.
• You don't see the silent struggles behind "smiling" selfies.

That girl with 100k followers? She might be battling loneliness. That boy flaunting abs? He might be dealing with pressure and body dysmorphia. You're not looking at a real person. You're looking at a performance.

Life Lesson: Your Worth Is Not Up for Debate

Read that again. Louder this time.

Let's get one thing straight, right here, right now:

You are not a trend. You are not a number. You are not an aesthetic.

Your worth isn't defined by how productive you were today, how smooth your skin is, how curated your feed looks, or how many people double-tapped your latest post. It's not about your "that girl" morning routine, your gym grind, your outfit, or how clean your notes look.

Your worth is not something you earn**. It's something you already have.**

From the minute you existed — messy, loud, weird, wonderful

— *You were already enough.*

You don't need to hustle for it. You don't need to pretty it up. You don't need to deserve it.

But the scroll doesn't let you remember that, does it?

Because every day, we're bombarded with messages telling us:

"You're almost enough... just fix this one thing."

"Glow-up first. Then you'll feel better."

"Buy this product. Change your face. Be more like her."

And without realizing it, we start shrinking ourselves to fit into invisible moulds.

More aesthetic. More productive. More filtered.

Less messy. Less loud. Less... us.

But guess what?

The most powerful thing you can be is real.

Take breaks from the scroll. Seriously. Put the phone down. Touch grass. Breathe. Paint something ugly. Dance like no one's recording a reel. Let yourself be fully in the moment — not thinking about how it'll look online. Curate your feed like you curate your playlist — with intention. Follow people who make you feel uplifted, not unworthy. People who make you want to live better, not smaller.

And most importantly:

Use your screen to **express**, not impress.

Post what makes you laugh.

Share your real thoughts, not just polished ones.

Be a chaos queen, a soft girl, a cottage core frog, a pink glitter bomb, a healing mess — whatever feels true.

Because here's the plot twist no influencer tells you:

The most beautiful life?
It's not the one you post.
It's the one you're present in.
The one where you laugh so hard your stomach hurts. The one where you cry, heal, grow, mess up, restart. The one where no one claps, but you're still proud of yourself. That's the life that matters.

So next time you start to spiral into the "not enough" narrative...

Pause.

Remind yourself:

Your worth is not up for debate. Not today. Not ever.

Sticky Note Reminder:

"You are allowed to exist without performing."

"Your life is enough, even if it's not aesthetic."

What Actually Matters?

Spoiler: It's not your follower count.

Let's flip the script for a second.

What if, instead of chasing likes, story views, or the perfect caption that hits just the right mix of deep and slay, we started chasing actual moments?

Not moments that look good online.
Moments that feel good — in your chest, in your bones, in your soul.

Like...

• Laughing so hard your stomach aches and your eyeliner smudges.
• Crying on the floor and then realizing, "Wait. I'm actually healing."
• That first sip of chai or coffee after a long, soul-sucking day.
• Making a playlist for someone who didn't even ask for one.
• Finishing a journal page, a painting, a poem — and thinking, "Dang. I made that."
• Sitting with a friend who gets your silence.
• Singing your favorite sad song at full volume with zero shame and all the windows down.
• Choosing yourself — again and again, even when it's hard.

Let's romanticize that.

Not the airport fit. Not the brunch shot. Not the "day in my life" that's more aesthetic than actual life.
Let's start chasing the *magic in the mess.*

The kind of joy that isn't performative — it's personal.
Because the truth?

Social media is a window, not a mirror. It can't reflect who you really are. It can't capture the galaxies you hold inside. Your thoughts. Your heart. Your weirdness. Your kindness. Your bad jokes. Your healing journey. The way your face lights up when you talk about something you love. None of that fits in a 15-second reel. *You are a whole galaxy. Social media can never capture all your stars.* You are not a highlight. You're the whole movie. You are not just a "vibe." You are a vibrant human being. You are not content. You are cosmic. So, if you've been feeling like your life doesn't measure up to the feeds you see... pause.
Put your hand over your heart.
Take a breath.
And ask yourself: **What actually matters to me?**
Because the likes fade. The algorithm forgets.
But you?
You're unforgettable.

Chapter 5

Setting Boundaries ≠ Being Mean

Let's get this straight—saying **"no"** doesn't make you rude, selfish, or a bad person. It makes you aware, brave, and in control of your energy.

The Guilt Trap

When "being nice" turns into self-betrayal. Let's talk about that one sneaky little emotion that quietly wrecks your boundaries like a wrecking ball with a smile:

Guilt.

Not the "oops, I ate all the fries" kind.

The "I said yes when I so badly wanted to say no" kind.

The "I guess I'll do it, even though I'm exhausted" kind.

The "I don't want to hurt their feelings... so I'll just hurt mine" kind.

Sound familiar?

Yeah. Same. I used to be *that girl.*

The "it's okay!!" girl.

The "don't worry about it :)" girl.

The "sure I can help even though I'm low-key dying inside" girl.

Would someone ask for a favor I didn't have time for? I'd say yes — instantly.

A friend would joke about something that actually hurt? I'd laugh it off — every time.

I'd go to hangouts I had no energy for, take calls when all I wanted was silence, and let people walk into my emotional space without knocking — because God forbid someone thought I was rude. Or selfish. Or "too much."

But guess what?

All that "niceness" didn't make me feel better.

It made me feel invisible in my own life.

Like I was starring in a movie where everyone else got the script — and I was just the background character with no lines, constantly saying "sure!" and "it's fine!" while screaming inside.

Here's the thing they don't tell you: Being kind doesn't mean being a doormat. Being chill doesn't mean being emotionally silent. Being a good friend doesn't mean erasing yourself. We're so conditioned to be "nice girls," "peacekeepers," "easy to be around," that we forget we're allowed to have limits. Boundaries aren't walls. They're doors. And not everyone deserves a key.

Saying no doesn't mean.

It's mature.

It's honest.

It's powerful.

You're not a villain for protecting your time, your peace, or your energy. You're not selfish for choosing yourself sometimes. You don't owe your comfort just because someone else asked nicely.

And if someone only likes you when you're constantly bending over backwards for them...

They don't like you.

They like your compliance.

Here's your permission slip (not that you needed one):

You can say no. You can leave the group chat on read. You can cancel plans. You can speak up. You can draw the line in bold, permanent marker.

Because the only person who has to live inside your body, mind, and soul — is you.

And you deserve to feel seen there.

The "Good Girl" Pressure

When society tells you to be soft, sweet, and silent — and you say, "Nah, I'd rather be real."

Let's get into it.

From the time we're little, teen girls — especially girls who are empathetic, emotional, or just deeply human — are told to be one thing above all else:

Nice.

Smile when someone interrupts you. Say thank you even when you feel uncomfortable. Don't speak too loudly. Don't take up too much space. Don't be dramatic. Don't be too opinionated. Be agreeable. Be cute. Be easy to like. Basically, be sugar-coated and small. And if you dare to say no, if you get firm with your boundaries, if you speak your truth or stop tolerating something that drains your soul... guess what the world suddenly calls you?

"Too much."

"Too emotional."

"Too intense."

"Difficult."

All because you decided to choose yourself.

I used to fall into this trap all the time. I'd say "yes" when I was tired. Laugh at jokes that hurt me because I didn't want to seem "too sensitive." Let people vent to me for hours, even when I was emotionally drowning, just so they wouldn't feel bad. All in the name of being "a good friend." All in the name of being nice.

But here's the twist no one tells you:

That kind of "good girl" energy doesn't make you feel good. It makes you feel invisible. It teaches you that your comfort doesn't matter as long as everyone else is comfortable. It teaches you to be liked... but not loved for who you truly are. It makes you available to everyone — but deeply disconnected from yourself. That's not kindness. That's quite self-abandonment.

Here's what they should've told us instead:

• Being kind doesn't mean being a people-pleaser.

• Being respectful doesn't mean staying silent.

• Being supportive doesn't mean sacrificing your sanity.

-And being "good" should never mean making yourself small just to make others feel big.

So, let's redefine what it means to be a "good girl," shall we?

A really good girl knows her worth — and doesn't water herself down. A really good girl listens, but also speaks. She shows up for others and herself.

She sets boundaries, says no, walks away when needed, and doesn't apologies for being a full human being with emotions, opinions, and limits.

Because real kindness includes being kind to yourself.

You don't have to be palatable. You don't have to be agreeable all the time. You don't have to twist yourself into someone else's comfort zone.

You can be soft and strong. You can be generous and grounded. You can be full of love without letting people take advantage of your light.

So, if you've ever felt guilty for speaking up...

If you've ever been called "too much" when you were just being honest...

If you've ever been scared that standing up for yourself would make people walk away...

Let them.

Anyone who leaves because you chose yourself was never rooting for the real you in the first place.

Being "nice" shouldn't cost you your voice. You don't owe anyone the version of you that makes them feel comfortable at your expense. You can be a good person without being a people-pleaser.

A Wake-Up Moment

I'll never forget when a friend of mine, Tara, asked me for money—again. It wasn't a lot, just a couple of hundred rupees, but I'd already given her some the month before. And this time, something inside me finally clicked. I hesitated and said gently, "I'm sorry, Tara. I don't think I can help this time."

She went quiet. Then cold. Started ignoring my texts, and I felt awful. I wondered—*was I a bad friend? Did I hurt her?*

That was the beginning of the end.
She stopped texting. Started hanging out with other girls. And when I saw her at school, she acted like I didn't exist. For days, I spiraled. I thought I had messed everything up. I replayed

that conversation in my head on a loop. I even drafted an apology text.

But before I hit send, I talked to a mutual friend—someone who quietly said, "You know she's borrowed from like three other people too, right? She never pays them back."

Boom. Perspective changed.

It wasn't me. It was her pattern.

I realized something: **Saying "no" had protected me. It had set me free.**

That moment taught me something huge: People who get mad at your boundaries are usually the ones benefiting from you not having any.

What I Learned from That

Boundaries don't make you mean—they make you safe. Tara wasn't a terrible person, but she was the kind of friend who took more than she gave. And I had every right to decide where I drew the line.

After that, I started practicing saying small "no's" in everyday life. It wasn't easy. My voice would shake, and sometimes I still felt guilty. But each time, I felt a little stronger. A little more me.

-A Simple Truth

Boundaries aren't walls to keep people out—

they're filters that help protect what's sacred inside you: your time, energy, peace, and joy. You teach others how to treat you by what you allow, what you stop, and what you walk away from.

Life Lessons (The Kinda Stuff School Never Taught Us)

• Your energy is a currency.
Spend it wisely — like your phone battery on 5%. You wouldn't open five apps, scroll through TikTok, and start a Netflix episode when your phone's dying, right? Same logic.

Don't drain your energy on people or situations that give you nothing back. Plug into things that recharge you — a walk, your favorite playlist, or just peace. Protect your vibe like it's your last bar of battery before bedtime.

• If someone leaves because of your boundary, they were never really for you.
People who genuinely care will respect your limits. If someone disappears the moment you stop overextending yourself — congratulations, the trash took itself out. Setting boundaries doesn't make you difficult; it makes you healthy. You're not supposed to shrink so others can feel

comfortable. The right ones will stay, and the wrong ones will ghost — both are answers.

• Saying "no" to others is sometimes saying "yes" to yourself.

"No" isn't rude. It's self-respect. Every time you turn down something that drains you, you create space for something that nourishes you — whether that's rest, joy, or a night in with snacks and self-care. Boundaries aren't walls; they're doors with locks only you have the key to. So go ahead, say "no" guilt-free — future you will thank you.

Real-Life Script:

You don't have to be aggressive to stand your ground. Here's how to say it calmly but clearly:

- "I'm not available for that right now."
- "I'm not comfortable discussing that."
- "That doesn't work for me, but thank you."

Remember: Clear is kind. Confusion is cruel.

Chapter 6

Comparison Kills Joy

"You can't bloom by staring at someone else's garden."

Let's talk about that weird little punch in the gut that happens when you see someone else winning, and instead of clapping, your heart sinks a little.

You're not even trying to feel that way. You want to be happy for them. You know they deserve it. But somehow... it makes you feel like you're falling behind.

Yeah. That's a comparison.

And it's brutal.

I remember this one evening so vividly. I was sitting cross-legged on my bed in my oldest, softest pyjamas — you know the ones that should've been retired three years ago. My hair was a mess. My thoughts were louder than usual. I was scrolling mindlessly, not looking for anything in particular — but somehow, I found exactly what would trigger my spiral.

Everyone on my feed seemed to be glowing. Sunset beach pictures. Group study dates. Glow-up selfies with "feeling grateful" captions. People were thriving. And me? I felt like I was wilting.

Then I saw Aanya's post. Now, Aanya wasn't just anyone. She was in my class. The girl who always had her hand up always had her life together. Every teacher's golden child.

Her caption read: "Honored to represent my state at the National Debate Championship. So grateful"

And just like that, the floor of my self-worth gave way. My chest felt heavy. My stomach twisted.

"What am I even doing with my life?"

Never mind that, that week I had helped a friend through a panic attack. Never mind that I'd written three full poems from the heart. Never mind that I was trying so hard to grow in my own quiet ways.

None of that felt like enough. Because her win felt like my failure. That night, I had a silent, solo cry. No dramatic sobbing. Just that numb, hollow ache that comes when your confidence starts to crumble quietly.

But somewhere in that moment, something clicked. I remembered this quote I'd once scribbled into a random notebook:

"Don't compare your behind-the-scenes with someone else's highlight reel."

And it hit me. Like, actually hit me. We don't see the chaos behind other people's curated posts. We don't see the nights they cry themselves to sleep. We don't see the pressure, the breakdowns, the fear, the messiness.

Social media is a performance. A filtered film.

It's the best 3 seconds of someone's entire 24 hours. Even Aanya — weeks later — opened up to me. She told me she felt like she was crumbling under the pressure to always be "on." That every win just made people expect more. And that sometimes, she just wanted to not be the "incredible one" for once.

And that's when I realized:

Even the people we think are living the dream? They're still trying to wake up from their own nightmares sometimes. So, I started slowly shifting.

• I unfollowed a few accounts that made me feel like I wasn't enough.
• I began noticing my own wins — no matter how tiny. Getting out of bed on a hard day? Win.
• Journaling my feelings instead of bottling them? Win.
• Smiling at my own reflection? Major win.

The comparison didn't vanish overnight. It still creeps in. But the joy? It started returning — in small, quiet, powerful ways.

Life Lesson: Your journey is yours — and that's your superpower.

Comparison is sneaky.

It doesn't knock on the door; it just slips into your mind when you least expect it. Maybe it's while you're scrolling through Instagram, seeing someone post their perfect vacation pictures. Maybe it's when your classmate announces an internship or job, and you're still figuring things out. Or maybe it's that quiet sting when a friend hits a milestone you thought you'd reach first.

And comparison? Oh, *it's dramatic.*

It whispers things like:
• *"You should be doing more."*

- *“Why aren’t you there yet?”*
- *“Everyone else is ahead of you.”*

And suddenly, instead of celebrating yourself, you're side-eyeing your own reflection like you’re behind in some invisible race.

But here’s the truth:

Someone else’s glow doesn’t dim yours. Their chapter 20 doesn’t invalidate your chapter 6. Their loud wins don’t erase your silent progress. You don’t have to catch up. You’re not behind. You’re simply on a different page in a completely different book.
Think about it: no one rushes a flower to bloom faster.
• Cherry blossoms bloom in spring—soft, delicate, here for a fleeting moment.
• Sunflowers wait for full sunlight and stand tall when it’s their season.
• Moonflowers bloom only at night, when the world is asleep, glowing in quiet secrecy.

And guess what? All of them are still breathtaking. So why do we forget this when it comes to ourselves?

Why do we think we need to copy someone else’s season when our own will come in time?

The world doesn't need seven billion identical success stories. It needs your story—told in your words, at your pace. If everyone bloomed at once, imagine how boring gardens would look. Your *"not yet"* doesn't mean *"never."*

Your progress counts, even when it's invisible to others, even when it's messy. Even when it's slow. Especially then.

Because **slow growth is still growth**.

And often, it's the kind that lasts the longest. So, the next time comparison sneaks in with its whispers, talk back to it.

Tell it:

"I'm not behind. I'm just building roots right now."

"I'm not late. I'm simply blooming in my season."

"I don't need to dim anyone else's light, because mine is on its way."

Trust your timing. Trust your path.

Trust the messy, magical process of becoming.

Because one day, you'll look back at all the times you thought you were "behind," and realize—

You were exactly where you needed to be.

Celebrate Others, Celebrate Yourself

Here's the thing: cheering for someone else doesn't mean you're booing yourself. We forget that sometimes, right? Like, your friend gets an internship, or someone you follow just bought their dream car, and suddenly your brain goes, *"Cool, but why am I still here?"* That's comparison sneaking in again. But honestly? Their glow doesn't switch off your light. It's not a competition—it's a playlist. You can love their song and still vibe with your own. Clapping for someone else doesn't silence your music; it just adds more sound to the celebration.

So instead of sulking in silence when someone else is thriving, try being the loudest cheerleader in the room. Hype them up. Throw confetti. Send the text that says, "I'm so proud of you, dude." You'll notice something crazy: celebrating others actually makes you feel lighter, not smaller.

But here's the catch—if you're always clapping for others and never for yourself, you'll start to run on empty. That's why you need a **"Proud of Me"** list. Not the fancy, Canva template, aesthetic notes-app thing you post for likes. No. I'm talking the raw, scribbled, slightly chaotic version. Things like:

- *"Got out of bed when I really didn't want to."*
- *"Actually, studied for 30 minutes without checking my phone."*
- *"Didn't cry over that text I didn't get."*
- *"Made myself chai and it was fire."*

Tiny things count. The kind of things you wouldn't even tell anyone else, but secretly? They matter the most. Because when you look back, you'll realize these "small wins" were actually the bricks you built your confidence on.

And let's be real: life isn't just about what looks good online. Likes aren't the same as joy. Followers don't guarantee peace. Aesthetic feeds don't mean someone's life is as perfect as their grid. What actually matters is what makes you feel alive.

Dancing like a complete dork in your room? *That's success.*
Laughing so hard your stomach hurts, and you forget what you were even sad about? *That's success.*
Writing a messy, weird little poem that only you understand? *That's success.*
Learning something random just because it made you curious? *Yup—success.*

You don't need a blue checkmark or a viral post to validate your life. Your moments of aliveness—the ones nobody even sees—are proof enough. So, here's the new vibe check:

- Hype others without dimming yourself.
- Clap for your own messy progress.
- Redefine success as anything that makes you feel alive.

Because at the end of the day, you're not just here to look like you're living. You're here to *actually live.*

Gentle Reminders:

- People post their wins, not their worries.
- Filters can cover skin, not sadness.
- Likes are not love.
- You don't need applause to prove that you're growing.

You don't need to become someone else's version of success. You don't need to bloom on demand. Your timeline, your pace, your passion — it's enough.

Because the world doesn't need another copy.

"It needs your kind of magic."

Chapter 7

"Why Am I Like This?" — The Anxiety Spiral We Don't Talk About

"It's not that deep." — But for you, it's kind of is.

You're lying on your bed, phone face down, playlist shuffling through sad songs as the algorithm *knows*, and you're staring at the ceiling like it might offer some sort of divine clarity.

Your chest feels tight. Not painful. Just... heavy.

There's this weird lump in your throat, but you're not crying. Your heart's beating a little too fast for someone who's just been horizontal for the past hour.

And what set it off?

You're not even sure.

Maybe it was the one text left on *"seen."* Or the weird look someone gave you in the hallway. Maybe it was that awkward thing you said *four days ago* that your brain randomly decided to dig up like a cringey fossil. Or maybe it's just... everything. All at once.

It's like your mind is a browser with 27 tabs open, and 3 of them are frozen, and you don't even know where the music is coming from. That's anxiety. And it doesn't always wear a label. It doesn't show up with warning signs or a heads-up.

Sometimes, it arrives dressed as *restlessness, as irritability, as* silence. As fake smiles and "I'm just tired". As a constant need to check your phone, or an overwhelming urge to toss it across the room.

And the worst part- people don't always get it.

"You're overthinking."

"It's not that deep."

"You're so dramatic."

But if it's keeping you up at 2 a.m., if it's making your hands sweat just to send a text, if it's replaying conversations on a loop like a broken podcast —

Then *yeah,* for *you*... It is that **deep**.

Story Time: The "Perfect" Girl with the Not-So-Perfect Brain

Meet Zara. She had it all together—or at least, that's what it looked like on Instagram.

Her feed? Immaculate.

Her grades? Always decent.

Her vibe? Cool, sarcastic, always "fine."

But no one knew about the silent battles she fought every single day. Like how she'd reread her texts 15 times before hitting send. Or how she'd cancel meetups last minute, claiming she was "busy," when in reality she was lying on her bed, spiraling.

She would get a weird stomach-ache every time someone said, *"We need to talk."*

And she'd cry in the shower, but joke about it like, "Haha, relatable, right?"

It all built up—until one day during lunch, a teacher casually said, *"You've been very quiet lately, Zara,"* and her throat tightened. She smiled and nodded, but inside she was drowning. Later that night, it all came crashing down.

She broke. The kind of break where no meme can fix it. Just sobbing. Tired. Confused. Angry at herself for *feeling too much.*

That was the moment she realized:

Anxiety isn't a drama. It's data.

Anxiety is not "just stress."

It was her mind waving a tiny flag saying: "Hey, I'm overloaded." Stress is a reaction to something specific — a test, a deadline, a presentation. Anxiety? It's the voice that whispers, *"But what if you mess up?"* even when nothing's technically wrong.

It's like your brain is always scanning for danger — even when you're safe.

You might look calm. You might even laugh at memes and show up to school or work like everything's fine. But inside, your mind's running laps. You're second-guessing every sentence.

Overanalyzing every emoji and wondering if your friends are slowly pulling away or if you're just being "too sensitive" again.

What Anxiety Really Is

-Spoiler alert: You're not broken. Your brain's just being a little... dramatic.

Imagine your brain is a phone. Now imagine there's this one app running in the background 24/7. You didn't open it. You didn't ask for it. But it's *there.* Constantly refreshing. Constantly draining your mental battery.

And worst of all? You can't delete it.

That's anxiety.

It's like your brain downloaded this glitchy survival software during childhood and forgot to run updates. Now it thinks that being *left on read,* tripping in public, or sending a "lol" without an emoji is an *existential threat.*

It's Not Drama. It's Your Nervous System.

Anxiety isn't about being "extra" or "too emotional."

It's literally your *fight-or-flight* system pulling the fire alarm... even when there's no fire. Just vibes. And maybe a passive-aggressive text. You're not being weak. Your body is just tired of pretending to be chill. Because pretending to be "fine" when you're not? That's *exhausting.*

Anxiety Feels Like...

- Your heart is sprinting while your body is just... sitting.
- Replaying one sentence from five days ago like it's your top Spotify track.
- Creating 17 worst-case scenarios from one harmless situation.

- Laughing in a group chat, then immediately wondering if they all secretly hate you.
- Getting a text and instantly assuming you did something wrong.

It's like your brain wants to protect you, but it doesn't know how to *relax.* So, it just throws red flags at everything — even a notification sound.

"Why Can't I Just Be Normal?" Ah, the classic spiral.

But here's the tea: *Normal doesn't exist.* Everyone's just masking different things. Some people overwork. Some people overshare. Some people people-please. Some people disappear.

You? You feel *deeply.* You sense danger where others don't. You analyze vibes like it's your part-time job. You're not weak. You're hyper-aware. You've been wired to protect yourself — sometimes at the cost of peace.

Fun Fact: Anxiety = Protection on Overdrive

Anxiety is your brain's overprotective friend. You know the one — she means well, but she's a bit much.

"What if they're mad at you?"

"Don't mess this up."

"Better rehearse that conversation in your head for the 38th time."

"Just stay quiet. It's safer."

She's not the enemy. She's just scared. And when you *understand* her, you can start softening her grip.

-Reminder:

You don't need to "fix" yourself.

You need to *understand* yourself.

Your anxiety isn't your identity.

It's not your whole personality.

It's just a system that's been working overtime — and now it needs a break, a snack, and maybe a nap.

"You're not broken. You're healing in real-time."

Real Ones Know:

- You can be bubbly and still have panic attacks.
- You can get good grades and still cry in the bathroom.
- You can be the "fun friend" and still feel like your mind is fighting itself.

• You can glow on Instagram and still spiral at night.

You are not your anxious thoughts. You are the soul *noticing* them. And that makes you *powerful.*

Healing Starts When You Say:

• "Actually, I'm not okay right now."
• "That made me feel anxious, and I don't know why, but I want to figure it out."
• "I need space."
• "I don't have the energy to talk, but I'd love some company."
• "I'm proud of myself for getting through today."

Self-Care for Anxious Minds (That's Not Just Bubble Baths):

• Set your phone to Do Not Disturb *without guilt.*
• Watch a comfort show you've seen 100 times (yes, again).
• Make a "what's true right now" list when your brain lies.
• Do *one* thing at a time — even if it's just brushing your hair.
• Take social media breaks like your mental health depends on it. (Because it does)

Real Talk: What It Can Look Like

• Overplanning convo in your head
• Feeling nervous in chill situations

- Thinking you annoyed everyone just by existing
- Being mentally tired after texting
- Telling yourself: *"Get over it,"* but not being able to

Sound familiar? That's anxiety. And it's more common than you think.

Tiny Lessons from a Big Feeling

Lesson 1: You're not "dramatic"—you're processing.

Your brain isn't betraying you. It's trying to protect you. Acknowledge it. Thank it. Then gently tell it: *"I've got this."*

Lesson 2: Rest is not optional.

Your mind needs downtime. You're allowed to do nothing and not feel guilty. Watch that silly show. Lie on the floor. Breathe.

Lesson 3: Triggers are teachers.

What makes you anxious might be showing you where healing is needed. Is it social pressure? Fear of failure? Comparison? Start noticing the pattern.

Lesson 4: You're not alone.

Even the most confident people you know have cried in the bathroom. Seriously. No one has it all together.

Let's Not Just Cope—Let's Care

• **Start small.** Make one choice that brings calm—even if it's just changing your ringtone to something soft.

• **Name it.** "This is anxiety talking." Labelling it creates distance.

• **Make a 'Safe Space List.'** People, songs, shows, foods, thoughts—whatever makes you feel grounded. Please Write it down. Use it when the wave hits.

• **Talk. With a friend.** With a therapist. Or even with your future self in a journal.

Chapter 8

"Good Vibes Only?" ... Nah, I'm Feeling Everything.

The Real Talk

You've seen it *everywhere.* Plastered on Pinterest boards. Hung in dorm rooms with fairy lights. Printed on water bottles, planners, and neon signs that scream things like:

"Good vibes only!"

"Stay positive."

"Just smile through the pain, bestie!"

Cute, right?

Aesthetic? Absolutely.

Helpful when your brain is doing backflips at 2 a.m.? ...Not so much.

Let's be **real:** when your heart feels like it's been drop-kicked down a staircase, when your thoughts won't shut up, and when you're running on empty but still trying to keep it together—Being told to "just think happy thoughts" feels like putting a glitter sticker on a broken bone. And that, my friend, is what we call **toxic positivity.**

It's this sneaky idea floating around everywhere that says:

"You're only strong if you're smiling."

"Don't talk about the heavy stuff. It ruins the vibe."

"Other people have it worse. Be grateful."

Ugh. Let's pause right there.

Can we all collectively agree that forcing a smile when you're crumbling inside is not strength? It's emotional gaslighting... but make it aesthetically pleasing.

Toxic positivity tells you that your pain is a problem—that it's too much, too messy, too dramatic. It teaches you to filter your feelings like an Instagram post:

Only show the highlights.

Only show the light.

Hide the shadows. Bury the chaos. Tuck it all in.

But here's the raw, unfiltered truth no one likes to post:

Sometimes, there is no silver lining, and sometimes life just sucks.

And *pretending* that it doesn't?

Doesn't make it suck less—it makes you feel more alone.

Because when you're told to "just stay positive," you start believing that feeling sad, angry, lost, or overwhelmed makes you weak or ungrateful. It doesn't.

It makes you human.

Let's Flip the Script

You don't have to smile when you're not okay. You don't have to "look on the bright side" when you're drowning. You don't have to be a walking inspirational quote when you're falling apart inside.

You're allowed to feel it all.

The good. The bad. The in-between. Real strength isn't in ignoring your emotions—it's in *owning* them.

So next time someone tells you "Good vibes only,"

You can hit 'em with:

"Nah, it's **real vibes only** over here."

You weren't made to be a robot with a permanent grin. You were made to be real, raw, and beautifully, messily human.

The Story: When "Just Be Positive" Hurt the Most

It was a regular Tuesday—but not *the cute coffee shop, tote bag, lo-fi playlist* kind of Tuesday. *Nope*. This one felt like my brain had 47 tabs open, and every single one was glitching.

I (Anshika) was hanging by a thread. Mentally, emotionally, even physically.

My exams-Total chaos.

My sleep schedule- Non-existent.

My emotions- All over the place, like a broken Google Map route with no destination.

I had reached that ugh, I can't make any more points. You know, when your chest feels tight, your eyes sting for no reason, and even replying "I'm fine" feels like a lie, you can't keep up anymore.

So, I did something bold. Scary, even.

I reached out and texted a friend, Someone I trusted, Someone I thought would get it.

I didn't pour my heart out. I just sent one simple, quiet message:

"Hey... I think I'm not okay."

I stared at the screen. Heart racing. Half-hoping they'd say "I'm here." Half-fearing I was being too much.

Then came the reply:

"Don't be sad! Just smile and move on. Everyone has bad days :)"

Smiley face and all. And just like that... boom.

My heart? Sunk.

My throat? Tight.

My brain? Instantly went: "Oh. Never mind."

It wasn't even meant to be mean. That's the worst part. They probably thought they were helping. But in that moment, their words hit harder than silence ever could.

It felt like I **wasn't** allowed to be sad.

Like, there was a timer on my feelings. Like, I was supposed to just snap out of it because... other people have it worse? Because "bad days" are normal?

So, I did what so many of us do:

I smiled. I replied, "Yeah, you're right." I slapped on the mask. Pretended I was fine. But inside? I felt like I was shrinking.

Like my emotions were *too heavy* for someone else's comfort. Like I had to fold myself into this quiet, convenient version of me just so I wouldn't make anyone uncomfortable.

And that night… I didn't cry because of the bad day. I cried because I felt *guilty*… for feeling.

Guilty for being vulnerable. Guilty for needing someone. Guilty for not being the "positive girl" everyone expected. I started thinking:

"Maybe I am too sensitive."

"Maybe I should stop opening up."

"Maybe people only like me when I'm 'happy' me."

And that's exactly what toxic positivity does. It tells you:

- Your sadness is too much.
- Your pain is inconvenient.
- Your emotions need to be filtered, toned down, muted.

It turns your real feelings into background noise. It makes you feel like you have to **apologies for being human.** But here's what I've learned since:

You are not too much. You were just too real for someone who only knew how to handle surface-level vibes.

Real Emotions > Fake Positivity

Here's a truth bomb:

Feeling your emotions is not a weakness. It's wisdom.

You were never meant to bottle up your sadness, ignore your anger, or bury your stress under a layer of fake smiles. You were meant to feel deeply and fully.

You were meant to explore the why behind your tears, your overthinking, your rage. Because buried emotions don't disappear—they pile up, until one day, they overflow in ways you can't control.

Let's stop pretending and start processing.

Life Lesson: Be Real with Yourself, Even If Others Can't Handle It

People will always be more comfortable with the "chill, happy" version of you.
But you don't exist just to be comfortable for others.
Your sadness isn't a glitch—it's a signal. Your anxiety isn't drama—it's your brain asking for care. Your mood swings don't make you weak—they make you human.

Real healing happens when you create space for your own emotions—even the uncomfortable ones. You don't need to slap a smile on your face to be lovable. You don't need to explain your low mood to make it valid. And you definitely don't need to be positive all the time to be worthy.
Here's your permission slip to feel it all:

Joy.
Rage.
Disappointment.
Excitement.
Loneliness.
Hope.
All of it belongs.
And *so do you.*

You can't grow if you keep skipping over your feelings. Real growth comes from sitting with your sadness, being curious about your anger, and gently asking your anxiety what it's trying to protect you from.

Feel it .Name it. Heal it.
Because pretending everything is fine doesn't make you strong. But feeling everything and still showing up? *That's magic.*

Real Talk: "Just Smile" Isn't Always the Answer

Sometimes, a smile is a strength. Sometimes, it's survival. But sometimes? It's a shield we use when the world makes us feel like our truth is "too intense."
And when people tell you to "just stay positive," what they're actually saying is:
"Your feelings make me uncomfortable, so can you please wrap them up in something prettier?"

It's not your job to make your emotions palatable for other people. You don't have to minimize your sadness to make someone else more comfortable. You don't have to fake your healing to keep being "likeable."

You deserve friends who respond with:
"Talk to me. I've got you."

"I'm not going anywhere."
"Let's sit with this together."
Because healing doesn't come from skipping over your feelings like a cringy TikTok transition. It comes from sitting with them. Naming them. Letting them breathe.
Even if it's messy. Even if it's loud. Even if it's not aesthetic.
If You've Ever Felt Dismissed... If you've ever opened up and felt brushed off, if you've ever regretted being honest because someone gave you a "motivational quote" instead of listening, if you've ever wondered whether your pain was too loud— Let me remind you:
You're not dramatic.
You're not weak.
You're not "too emotional."
You're just honest.
And honest people shake things up. Your emotions are not a burden. They're a message. And you don't need to mute yourself to belong.

Tiny Reminder

"You can be grateful and tired.

You can be blessed and overwhelmed. You can be magical and messy.

You are not here to be a sunshine robot. You are here to be real."

Chapter 9

FOMO vs. JOMO

The Story: "Everyone Was There... Except Me"

It was a Saturday night, the kind of night where the world feels alive. Somewhere out there, music was thumping, people were laughing, and lights were glowing like little galaxies. But not in my room.

My room was quiet, lit only by the dim glow of my phone. I was sprawled on my bed in my soft pyjamas, the ones with little cartoon clouds on them, hair tied up in the messiest bun of my life, blanket twisted around my legs. Honestly, I was fine at first—just bored, doing my usual scroll-through-Instagram routine.

But then, the stories started rolling in.

The first one looked harmless enough: Riya's selfie. Except it wasn't harmless. She looked *perfect—sparkly* filter, highlighter shining like she was dipped in fairy dust, that pouty smile that said, "I know I look amazing and you wish you were here."

I tapped again.

Arjun's story.

The camera shook with bass, colors flashing neon, people jumping up and down like they didn't have exams on Monday. I could almost hear the thump of the music vibrate inside my chest through the tiny speakers.
Tap again.

Meher's boomerang.
Everyone—literally everyone—clinking glasses, wide grins, glitter eye shadow, sparkly eyeliner catching the light, hair shining like shampoo commercials. The caption?

Nights like these

My heart?
Straight into my stomach.
I wasn't there. Not in the background. Not tagged. Not even mentioned.
And suddenly, my brain flipped into panic mode.

"Why wasn't I invited?"

"Did I do something wrong?"

"Are they sick of me? Did I say something? Am I... too boring?"

It was like my thoughts were racing each other, tripping over themselves to reach the finish line of *self-doubt.*

I thought back to yesterday, that moment in school where they were whispering and giggling, saying something about "tomorrow." I had brushed it off, telling myself, It's *probably nothing*. But here was the proof: it wasn't nothing. It was everything. And everything didn't include me.
I kept tapping through their stories like I was watching a movie I didn't buy a ticket for. The hugs. The sparkly confetti filters. The laughing-so-hard-you-fall-on-the-floor kind of clips. The exaggerated "best night ever" captions.

And here's the thing—logically, I knew it was just a party. Just one night. But in that moment, it didn't feel like "just." It felt like the entire world was out there living their best lives, while I was stuck at home, invisible.

I even checked Snapchat again, like maybe I'd missed something. Maybe they'd sent me a last-minute invite, and I just didn't see it. Or maybe someone had tagged me in a story, and I'd somehow skipped past it. My fingers were trembling, scrolling, refreshing, desperate. But nope. Nothing. Just silence.

And that silence was louder than the music in their videos.
The sadness started small, like a little lump in my throat. But then it grew. My chest tightened. My stomach dropped. My heart actually hurt—like physically hurt. And then came the tears. At first, just one. Then two. Then a flood.

Ugly crying. Pillow-soaking crying. The kind where you feel embarrassed even though no one can see you. The kind where you ask yourself:

"Why am I never enough?"
"Why do I always end up on the outside?"
"Why does it feel like everyone else belongs except me?"

I clutched my phone to my chest like it held the answers to who I was. But all it gave me was more proof that I didn't belong. Every glowing screen, every filter, every laugh—they were having the time of their lives. And me? I was just... here. Alone.

I tried distracting myself. Opened YouTube. Scrolled Pinterest. Even googled "movies to watch when you're sad." But no matter what I did, the party was still playing in the back of my head like a song on repeat.

At one point, I actually debated texting someone. A simple "Hey, what's up?" to see if anyone would notice me. But I didn't. Because what if they didn't reply? Or worse, what if they replied with, "Busy at the party!"

That would've shattered me completely.

So, I didn't text. I just stared at my screen until the battery warning popped up. Then, finally, I gave up. Threw my phone under the blanket as it had betrayed me, buried my face in my pillow, and let the tears run until they stopped on their own. Somewhere out there, laughter echoed. Music played. Glasses clinked. But not here.
Here, it was just me, my blanket, and the echo of every insecurity I'd ever had.
And the worst part wasn't that I wasn't at the party.
The worst part was the thought that maybe... maybe I didn't belong anywhere at all.

Let's Talk About It: The FOMO Trap

We've all been there. That sharp, ugly sting in your chest when you realize something fun, something Instagram-worthy, something that everybody's talking about—is happening without you.

It doesn't even matter if you were fine five minutes ago. The second you see that glowing story, that group photo, that one post with the caption "Best night ever," it's like your mood free-falls straight through the floor.

And here's the part that hurts the most: it's not really about the party or the dinner or the trip. It's about what those things seem to represent.

FOMO is sneaky like that. It whispers in your ear things like:

- "You're not important enough to be invited."
- "Everyone else is making memories without you."
- "Your life is boring compared to theirs."
- "You don't matter as much as you thought you did."

And suddenly, you're not just missing out on an event—you feel like you're missing out on belonging.

The Social Media Effect

Now, let's add social media into the mix.

It's like pouring glitter over your insecurities—suddenly everything looks shinier, sparkler, and way more perfect than it really is.

You scroll, and what do you see?

• Perfect group selfies.
• Laughter frozen in boomerangs.
• Captions like "Nights like these" or "My people, my world."
• Filters that make everyone's skin glow as they live in a commercial.

But here's the truth: *"social media is a highlight reel, not a documentary."*

Nobody's posting about the fight they had with their parents before leaving the house. Nobody's showing how awkward they felt when they didn't know what to say at the party. Nobody's recording the moment they cried in the bathroom because *they felt left out, even while being there.*

They're posting the best 5% of their lives. The curated, polished, share-worthy bits. The other 95%? The boredom, the anxiety, the insecurities, the loneliness? It's still there—it just doesn't make the feed.

And that's what FOMO feeds on. It makes you compare your behind-the-scenes to someone else's highlight reel. And of course, you're going to feel like you're losing.

The Belonging Question

But here's something most people don't say but loudly:

Being left out doesn't mean you're unworthy. Sometimes, it's just logistics. Maybe the group was small. Maybe there were space issues. Maybe it was last-minute. And sometimes... the space simply wasn't meant for your magic.

And that's okay.

Not every room deserves your presence. Not every party needs your energy. Not every group can handle the uniqueness you bring. Your worth isn't tied to whether or not you show up in someone else's story—it's tied to who you are when no one's watching.

The Universal FOMO

And here's the sneakiest truth of all: the people who look like they're "living it up"? They feel FOMO too.
The girl posting flawless selfies? She's probably comparing herself to someone else's trip to Goa.
The guy flexing his night out? He might be sitting in an Uber later, wishing his life looked like his favorite influencer's.
Even the group that left you out? They probably scroll too, feeling that same hollow ache about someone else's "perfect" life.

FOMO is universal. It doesn't mean something's wrong with you—it means you're human.

The Trap

FOMO wants you to believe that:

- you're behind,
- you're unloved,
- and your life is less exciting.

But the truth? You're not behind. You're exactly where you need to be.
You're not unloved. You're just not meant to be loved by everyone—and that's normal.
And your life? It doesn't need to be a highlight reel. It just needs to feel real to you.

Because at the end of the day, FOMO is just a trap. A trap that pulls you away from your own joy and convinces you that your worth lives in someone else's story. But it doesn't. It never has.
You're Not Missing Out, You're Being Redirected

Here's the thing nobody tells you when FOMO punches you in the gut: that ache in your chest isn't really about the party, or the dinner, or the late-night hangout. It's about what those things seem to mean. You feel like you weren't chosen. Like you didn't matter enough to make the list. Like the world is spinning without you on it.

But what if I told you—**you're not actually missing out? You're just being redirected.**

Think of it like Google Maps. You wanted one route, but it says "rerouting" and sends you another way. Annoying? Yes. But sometimes the alternate path is smoother, safer, or even leads you somewhere better. Being left out doesn't equal rejection. Sometimes, it's divine protection.

Pause & Ask Yourself

Instead of spiraling into the "I'm not good enough" cycle, hit pause. Ask yourself:

- **"What am I really feeling right now?"** Am I lonely? Do I feel rejected? Or is this about my own insecurity popping up again? Naming the monster makes it way less scary.
- **"Would I even have loved being there?"** Be brutally honest. Would you have thrived, or would you have been the quiet one in the corner, checking your phone every 10 minutes?
- **"Am I showing up for myself the way I keep begging others to show up for me?"** Sometimes we crave validation from others because we've been neglecting our own needs. When you look deeper, you realize this: sometimes being left out isn't a punishment—it's an opportunity.

It creates space for things you actually need:

• **More authentic friendships** — the ones where you don't have to beg for a seat at the table, because the table was built for you.

• **Discovering your own passions** — maybe it's painting, writing, binge-reading fantasy books, or even building playlists that feel like therapy.

• **Learning joy on your own terms** — the kind of joy that isn't dependent on who texts you or tags you.

That's not "missing out." That's rerouting your energy to something real.

The Flip: From FOMO → JOMO

We all know FOMO by now. That gut-sinking, tear-prickling, stomach-churning feeling when you see everyone out laughing, vibing, living their best life™, while you're... what? A human blanket burrito with crumbs on your shirt, scrolling like, "Cool, I guess my life is over."

But what if—plot twist—that wasn't tragic? What if that was actually kind of... beautiful?

Enter:

#JOMO — The Joy of Missing Out.

JOMO is when you realize: *Wait a second... I'm not missing out. I'm saving myself from chaos.*

Think about it:

• You're dodging drama disguised as "fun."
• You're skipping the glitter fallout that will never come out of your hair.
• You're avoiding the awkward small talk with people who still mispronounce your name.
• You're safe from that one person who cries after two sodas and tells everyone's secrets.

Instead, you're at home. Cozy. Free. Snacks within reach. Music you actually like playing. No pretending. No exhausting energy drain. Just you, being you. And that's not "boring." That's sacred.

The Unseen Side

Here's the real tea no one posts:

• Someone at that party? They cried in the bathroom because they felt left out while being there.
• Someone else got dragged into messy drama and went home with regrets.
• And someone stood in the corner pretending to text, wishing they were literally anywhere else.

But you'll never see that in stories. Because social media is a highlight reel, not the full movie. And you? You're comparing your messy behind-the-scenes (the snacks, the PJs, the unwashed hair bun) to someone else's heavily edited trailer. Of course, it looks shinier—it's designed to.

The Secret Power of JOMO

The real flex isn't being everywhere, doing everything, knowing everyone. The real flex is being so at peace with yourself that you don't need constant proof that you belong.

JOMO is the reminder that:

• You're not falling behind. You're right on time.
• You're not unloved. You just don't need everyone's love to be valuable.
• You're not invisible. You're just choosing not to measure your worth in likes, invites, or glitter-filtered stories.

Peace is underrated. Solitude is powerful. And sometimes, staying home in your silly socks, sipping chai, and laughing at your own dumb memes is the truest kind of joy there is.
Because you're not missing out.
You're just making room.

And trust me—what you're making room for is so much better than forcing yourself into a space where you were never meant to fit.

JOMO Era Feels Like:

• Saying "nope" to plans without guilt and realizing the world didn't actually end.
• Slurping instant noodles at midnight like it's a five-star meal.
• Rearranging your room at 2 AM just because you felt like it.
• Putting your headphones on and dancing around your room like you're in a music video no one else gets to see.
• Taking the longest shower ever and pretending you're in one of those dramatic shampoo commercials.
• Doodling random squiggles that somehow turn into your next masterpiece.
• Walking to the corner shop for ice cream in pyjamas because who's gonna stop you?
• Laughing at your own jokes while sprawled on your bed like the main character of your own indie film.
• Taking silly selfies that never hit Instagram but live forever in your camera roll.
• Realizing that your joy doesn't need witnesses — it just needs you.

Example?

FOMO says:

"Omg, everyone's at that rooftop party. What if I never get invited again?"

JOMO says:

"It's raining, I've got hot chocolate, a comfort show on, and zero energy to fake-smile. I win."

Reminder From Your Chill Era:

You're not behind. You're not boring. You're not missing out on life — you're curating *your own version of it.*

Joy isn't always loud. Sometimes, it looks like:

- Saying no to things that drain you
- Choosing comfort over chaos
- Laughing at memes under a blanket
- Journaling at 2 AM because your mind is racing
- Resting. Healing. Breathing.

Your timeline is yours. You don't have to keep up with everyone else's.

-Life Advice:

When FOMO strikes, ask yourself:

- Would I actually enjoy that event, or am I just afraid of being left out?
- What do I need right now — rest, recharge, or reconnect?
- Am I chasing connection or just reacting to pressure?

The real flex?

Being so in love with your own life that you don't care what's trending. You're not missing out.
You're choosing peace over pressure. And honestly? That's iconic.

Chapter 10

It's Complicated

Story Time: "Are We… Something?"

Ananya had been talking to Aarav for three months straight — and not in the casual, *"hey, what's up?"* kind of way. This was the good morning texts before breakfast, the goodnight pings after brushing teeth kind of consistency.

They shared memes all day. They played songs for each other over calls. They even FaceTime at night until one of them drifted off mid-conversation, the phone slowly sliding from their hand onto the pillow.

Aarav noticed the tiniest things: when Ananya wore her new scrunchie, when she changed her display picture, when she posted a random aesthetic story at 2 a.m. He even dropped those magical-sounding lines like:

"You're different from everyone else."

(Spoiler alert: he probably recycled that line for every other person on his chat list, too.)

Ananya, meanwhile, started living in two parallel worlds. In one, she was the fun, chill teen laughing with her friends. In the other, she was glued to her phone, waiting for Aarav's notifications, overthinking every reply like it was part of an exam paper.

Should she send "lol"? Or "ha-ha"? Or just the emoji with sparkles? What if "lol" made her sound boring? What if "ha-ha" made her sound too eager?

Every time his name flashed across her screen, her stomach did gymnastics worthy of an Olympic medal.

But here's the problem — there was no clarity.

No, "this is what we are."

No certainty.

Just... vibes floating in the air.

Whenever Ananya tried to gently bring it up, Aarav was the master of dodging.

"Why spoil what's working perfectly?" he'd say, tilting his head with that practiced smirk.

And if she asked again? Aarav would suddenly disappear like a magician's trick — no texts, no calls, total silence for two to three business days.

Yet, the moment Ananya posted a picture with another guy, Aarav transformed into Sherlock Holmes with a side of jealousy.

"Who's that?"

"Why's he standing so close?"

"Oh, so you've already moved on?"

Confusing? Absolutely.

Frustrating? Beyond words.

And just when Ananya decided, *That's it. I'm walking away,* Aarav would drop the ultimate *"pull you back in"* one-liners:
"I miss you."
"You just... get me."
"You're my peace."

And just like that, Ananya's determination would melt quicker than ice cream in a Delhi summer.

The truth? Ananya was stuck in what people call a **situationship.**

She was giving her emotions, her time, her energy — as if she was in something solid. But in reality? She was standing on quicksand.

It wasn't anything.

But it wasn't something either.

And that messy middle? It drained her even more than an actual ending would have. Because with an ending, at least you know what you're letting go of. But here, Ananya was left grieving something that never really existed in the first place.

One evening, Ananya sat staring at her phone, waiting for Aarav's reply.

One tick. Two ticks. Blue ticks. No answer.

Classic Aarav.

Meanwhile, her assignments sat unfinished, her friends were blowing up the group chat, and her favorite show had dropped a new episode. But here she was, frozen, holding her breath over a maybe.

That's when it hit her: Aarav was like a bus that always said it was coming... but never actually showed up. And she? She was the one standing at the bus stop, wasting time, when she could've just walked, taken another ride, or honestly... stayed home and chilled.

She thought back to the effort she put in: remembering his football practice schedule, hyping him up before his tests, listening to his rants about teachers. But when she needed him?

Ghost town. Aarav was basically like Wi-Fi that only worked when he needed it. Unstable, unreliable, and always dropping at the worst possible moment.

That night, Ananya wrote in her journal:

"If he wanted to choose me, he already would have. I don't need to beg for clarity. I deserve to be someone's priority, not their backup plan."

And for the first time in weeks, she slept without waiting for his "goodnight." No cartwheels in her stomach, no overthinking texts, no hanging on to half-answers. Just... peace.

Because the truth was simple: Ananya realized she wasn't asking for too much. She was just asking the wrong person.

What We Can Learn from Ananya's Story

Here's the thing: Ananya's story isn't just hers. A lot of teens go through the same kind of "half-connection" where you're giving so much of your time and emotions, but the other person never really gives you clarity.

And here's the secret: it's not about Aarav at all. It's about realizing what you deserve.

Think of it this way:

- Would you keep playing a video game that never lets you unlock the next level, no matter how many hours you put in? Probably not.
- Would you keep standing in the lunch line if the person serving food kept ignoring your plate? Definitely not.
- So why keep waiting for someone who enjoys your energy but never actually chooses you fully?

That's the trap of a situationship — it feels like something, but in reality, it's just enough to keep you hooked, not enough to make you secure.

What Ananya realized — and what you can too — is that asking for honesty, effort, and clarity is not "too much." It's the *bare minimum.*

You don't need to beg for consistency. You don't need to keep decoding mixed signals like they're math word problems. And you definitely don't need to waste your energy waiting for someone who disappears whenever things get real.

Because here's the truth no one tells you:

The right people don't leave you guessing. They make you feel safe, seen, and steady.

So, if you ever find yourself in Ananya's shoes — smiling at your phone but secretly drained inside

— take a step back and ask: *"Am I really happy, or am I just holding on to what I wish this could be?"*

You deserve connections that don't just sparkle in the beginning, but stay solid all the way through.

The Roast Session

One evening, sitting with her best friends over a plate of peri-peri fries, Ananya finally vented.

"So basically," she sighed dramatically, "I'm like... his unofficial girlfriend. Like an unpaid intern in the corporate office of his love life."

Her friends nearly choked on their drinks.

"Babe," said Riya, trying not to laugh, "you're literally in a trial version of a relationship. No commitment, just free features."

"Yeah," added Mehak, "except the free trial keeps auto-renewing and you can't find the cancel button."

They all burst into laughter, but Ananya felt the truth sting. Aarav gave her just enough to keep her hooked, but never enough to give her peace.

And that was the moment she realized — a situationship isn't really *complicated*. It's just one-sided.

What Even Is a Situationship?

A situationship is like being stuck in the middle of a game without knowing the rules. You're not "just friends," but you're also not in something steady. You're floating in a confusing in-between zone — the grey area of modern connections.

It feels like this:

You're giving someone your time, your attention, your energy — the kind of effort you'd give to someone really special. You share jokes, late-night chats, secrets, and maybe even daily check-ins. On the outside, it looks like something real. To everyone else, it might even seem like the two of you have something going on.

But here's the catch — there's no clarity. No steady ground to stand on. No clear answer when you ask yourself, *"So... what exactly are we doing here?"* You keep waiting for them to explain, to name it, to make it clear — but the clarity never comes.

That leaves you in a strange space: sometimes happy, sometimes anxious, always second-guessing. You're left wondering: *Do they actually value me, or do they just like the attention I give them? Am I really important, or just convenient?*

Everyday Analogies

Being in a situationship is a lot like starting your homework but never handing it in. You've put in the effort, stayed up late, scribbled down every answer — but because it never gets submitted, you don't get any recognition or results. It feels like all your energy is going into something that never counts for anything.

It's also like having Wi-Fi that only works when it feels like it. Some days, the connection is strong and smooth, and you think, yes, finally! But then it cuts out suddenly, leaving you frustrated and stuck in the middle of your favorite video. You can't rely on it, no matter how much you want to.

Or imagine playing the same level of a video game again and again. At first, it's fun and exciting. But when you realize, you're never allowed to unlock the next level, it becomes tiring. You keep putting in hours, but you're not actually getting anywhere.

A situationship can even feel like lending someone your favorite hoodie. They wear it all the time, enjoy the comfort, and never want to give it back. But they also don't treat it with the care it deserves — leaving you feeling like your effort isn't valued.

And maybe the clearest picture: it's like waiting at a bus stop for a bus that never arrives. You stand there with hope, checking your watch, holding onto the idea that "maybe it's coming soon." But deep down, you know the bus was never going to show up in the first place.

That's why situationships can feel so exhausting. They give you just enough to keep you waiting, but never enough to give you peace. You're always left hanging — half-happy, half-confused — and that half-hearted space drains you more than being fully in or fully out ever could.

How It Feels Inside

At first, a situationship can feel magical. Your phone lights up, and it's them. Suddenly, your day feels a little brighter. They notice the small things about you — your new haircut, the way you doodle in your notebook, the funny captions you post. That kind of attention makes you feel special, like you're seen in a way no one else notices.

It's exciting. You get butterflies every time a message pops up. You start waiting for their replies, even planning your day around when you'll talk. It feels like you've found someone who gets you — someone who makes even the most ordinary day feel lighter.

But then, slowly, the excitement turns into questions.

Why do they disappear sometimes when you need them most?

Why do they avoid giving clear answers when you try to figure out what this is?

Why does their attention feel so strong one day and so distant the next?

That's when the confusion sets in. Your mind starts racing at night — did you say something wrong? Are you being too much? Too little? You keep replaying conversations, overanalyzing emojis, and wondering if their silence means something. Instead of feeling calm, you're left restless.

And then comes the hardest part — the drain. You've given your energy, your time, your heart-space, but you're not getting the same back. It feels like pouring water into a bucket with a hole in it. No matter how much you give, it never fills.

In the end, being in a situationship isn't just about "liking someone." It's about the toll it takes on you. The constant waiting. The endless guessing. The cycle of hope and letdown. It's like riding a rollercoaster that never stops — exciting at first, but eventually, it just makes you dizzy and tired.

That's why it's so important to recognize it early. Because you deserve steadiness, not endless uncertainty.

How to Spot a Situationship Early

Here's the thing: situationships rarely *start* confusing. In the beginning, everything feels fun and effortless — the long chats, the inside jokes, the little compliments. It feels good, so you don't really stop to ask deeper questions.

But after a while, you notice patterns. Maybe you keep giving your time and attention, but when you need the same energy back, it's not there. Maybe they keep you close enough to feel special, but far enough that you never feel secure. Maybe every time you try to talk about where things are going, they dodge, laugh it off, or disappear for a while.

These are not accidents. They're signs.

Signs that you're putting your heart into something that doesn't give you the same comfort back. Signs that you're being treated like a "maybe," when you deserve a clear "yes."

What It Does to You

The hardest part about a situationship is not what the other person does — it's what it makes you do to yourself. You start doubting your worth, wondering if you're asking for too much. You replay conversations at night, editing yourself in your head. You stay even when you're tired, hoping maybe one day they'll see your value clearly.

It can eat up your peace of mind quietly. One day, you wake up and realize you've been waiting for answers that were never going to come. That's the draining part — not knowing what you are, or where you stand.

How to Protect Your Energy

The truth is, you can't control how someone else treats you. But you can control how much access they get to you. If someone keeps you in confusion for too long, step back. Protect your time, your thoughts, and your peace.

Remember: attention is not the same as care.

Messages are not the same as effort.

Consistency matters more than sweet words.

You deserve clarity. You deserve steadiness. You deserve connections where you don't have to keep guessing.

So, if you ever find yourself in a situationship, know this: walking away isn't losing something — it's making space for better, healthier connections that don't leave you drained.

Why It Feels So Pressuring

When you're in your teens, it can feel like the whole world is whispering: "Hurry up. Find someone. Don't be left out."

On social media, it's everywhere. Scrolling through your feed, you see people holding hands, writing long captions about "their person," or doing those viral couple dances. It looks picture-perfect, like everyone has already found their forever match while you're still figuring out what to eat for lunch. Even though deep down you know it's often staged, it still gets into your head.

From friends and peers, the pressure sneaks in differently. Maybe someone teases, "Wait, you've never had a crush before?" or "You don't talk to anyone like that?" It's meant as a joke, but it plants a seed that makes you question yourself: Am I behind? Am I missing out? Suddenly, something that wasn't even on your mind starts to feel urgent.

Then there are movies and music. Almost every song on the radio, every series on Netflix, every movie poster in the mall seems to scream the same message: love equals happiness. The main characters always find someone, and the story makes it look like life only gets magical once you do, too. It's easy to believe that your own story should look the same.

And finally, the most powerful pressure is the one that comes from **inside you**. It's natural to want to feel special, noticed, and chosen. You start wondering what it would feel like to have someone check in on you, to save you a seat, to notice the little things that others miss. That longing isn't silly — it's human. But when you're still learning who you are, that desire can feel like it's pulling you faster than you're ready to go.

All these voices together can make you rush. They can make you say yes to something unclear, confusing, or one-sided — just so you won't feel left out. But here's the truth: settling for half-effort, half-truth, or half-care doesn't fill the emptiness. In fact, it leaves you feeling lonelier than before, because now you've given pieces of yourself to someone who didn't really value them.

That's why it's important to pause. To ask yourself*: Am I choosing this because I truly want it, or because I feel like I'm supposed to?*

Because the pressure is real — but so is your power to say, *"Not yet. Not like this."*

A Heart-to-Heart Reminder

Wanting clarity doesn't make you needy. It makes you human. When you care about someone, it's natural to want to know where you stand. You are not asking for "too much" when you hope for honesty, consistency, or effort. Those are the basics — not extras.

Here's what you deserve: energy that matches yours, respect that doesn't waver, and effort that doesn't need constant reminding. You shouldn't have to beg for these things or feel guilty for wanting them.

A situationship isn't a gentle step toward something real. Most of the time, it's a shortcut someone takes to enjoy the benefits of your attention without giving back the same commitment. It's like playing a game where only one person follows the rules, while the other just makes them up as they go.

And the simplest truth is this: if you're confused all the time, it's not because you missed a sign. It's because they're not giving you clarity. Genuine care doesn't make you overthink; it makes you feel safe and steady.

Love — the real kind — is not meant to be a constant puzzle where you're left guessing. It's not supposed to drain you, make you anxious, or leave you second-guessing your worth. The right connections bring calm, not chaos.

So, here's your gentle reminder: you are worthy of clarity, honesty, and peace. Don't settle for anything that feels like half-truths or half-effort.

Because you're not a backup battery to be used when someone else's energy runs out. You're the main source of light — steady, bright, and powerful on your own. Anyone who steps into your world should only make that light shine even more; never dim it.

Life Lesson: Choose Yourself First

Let's make one thing clear: Your worth isn't measured by whether someone "likes" your back.

You are whole on your own. You don't need a title to feel valuable.

In fact, the best relationships often start when you know your value so deeply, you don't settle for almost.

- Almost love
- Almost loyal
- Almost committed

Walk away from the almost. You're made for always.

"If it's making you question your worth daily, it's not a vibe — it's a red flag."

Chapter 11

Love Doesn't Always Speak the Same Language

Because wanting to be understood doesn't make you ungrateful.

The Quiet Distance

Sometimes, it's not the big fights that hurt the most.

It's the silence.
The sighs.
The *"you've changed."*

The quiet space between what you *feel and what they want.*

You might be growing into your own opinions, discovering your identity, exploring your creativity — and suddenly, it feels like you're speaking a different language than your parents. You're trying to express you... And they're trying to protect you. But somehow, it feels like they're protecting you from yourself.

The Struggle Is Real

Sometimes, the people who love us the most don't always understand us the best. You try to open up about your dreams, your identity, or your mental health — and instead of being embraced, you're met with confusion, worry, or a lecture that starts with:

"We just want what's best for you."

And they mean it. But sometimes*, their* version of "best" doesn't match yours.

Story Time — Realization

Ria was the perfect daughter on paper. Tidy room. Top grades. Never skipped class. But underneath all that, obedience was someone
craving to breathe freely. She didn't want to be a doctor, like her dad. She didn't dream of IIT or medical coaching or lab coats.

She wanted to create worlds. Sketch characters. Tell stories that make people *feel.*

But the more she tried to talk about it, the more her parents shut down.

"You want to waste your future?"

"What will people say?"

"There's no money in that."

"You'll thank us later."

They weren't cruel. They weren't abusive. They were scared. Scared she would get hurt by a world that doesn't always reward passion. Scared their daughter wouldn't be "safe" if she strayed from the traditional path.

And Ria? She started feeling like she was selfish for dreaming. Like she was wrong for not wanting what they wanted. Like she was *disrespectful* for wanting more.

Until one day, she stopped asking for permission — and started asking for a *conversation.*

She showed them her sketchbook. Her YouTube channel. Her little animation reel. And she said, with tears in her eyes:

"I know you're scared. But this is who I am. I need you to trust that I won't give up on myself. Just like you never gave up on me."

It didn't magically fix everything. But it softened something. They still didn't get all of it — but they started to try.

That mattered.

Life Lesson:

Your parents aren't villains in your story — they're humans navigating life with the lessons, experiences, and fears that shaped them, and even when their actions or words feel frustrating, limiting, or confusing, it doesn't mean they love you any less; it just means they are doing their best with the tools they have. They grew up in a world that often said, *"Follow the rules. Stay quiet. Don't take risks. Pick the safe path. Don't stand out. Don't question authority,"* and those messages influenced everything they believe about right and wrong, success and failure, safety and freedom. Because of that upbringing, they sometimes struggle to understand your world — a world that is faster, louder, more colorful, and full of possibilities they never imagined for themselves. And that's okay. Their love might show up as worry, rules, or advice that feels restrictive, but it comes from a place of care, even if it doesn't always match your feelings, needs, or ambitions. Wanting to be seen, heard, and understood doesn't make you dramatic, spoiled, or rebellious — it makes you human. It makes you the narrator of your own story, the main character in a life that is messy, magical, and yours alone to shape, and sometimes that story looks very different from theirs.

You're allowed — and even expected — to grow into someone they may not fully understand yet. You are allowed to make decisions that challenge their expectations, to experiment, to stumble, to follow paths they didn't take, and to express yourself in ways they might initially resist or question. For example, maybe you've decided to pursue art, dance, writing, or something unconventional that makes your parents nervous. Maybe you're spending time with friends who don't fully get you, or expressing your personality in ways that feel bold or messy to them. That's okay. Sometimes love looks like fear, rules sound like walls, freedom sounds like rebellion, and what feels like criticism is just their imperfect attempt to guide you. That doesn't diminish the bond you share; it just means the storylines between you and them are different, and learning to respect both your path and theirs is part of growing up.

I remember a friend, Ankita, who wanted to join the school theatre club. Her parents were supportive in theory, but worried about grades, time, and "what other people would say." Every audition, every rehearsal felt like a negotiation between her dreams and their expectations. She loved performing, but she also loved her parents' approval. For months, she struggled with guilt and frustration, wondering if she could really follow her passion without disappointing them. It took a long time for her to realize that her growth didn't erase their love — it just meant she was claiming her story. When she finally performed in the school play, she was nervous, exhausted, and exhilarated. Her parents were in the audience, some frowning at first, but by the end, they were clapping, proud of her, and she realized that love doesn't always start with understanding; sometimes it starts with patience, with witnessing, with allowing space to grow.

Every teenager has moments like this. Maybe you've argued with your parents over small things like phone rules, clothes, or social media use. Maybe they've pushed you to study when all you wanted was to draw or write or take a mental health day. Maybe they've told you, "You'll understand when you're older", or "we know what's best for you." It can feel suffocating, like they don't see you at all. And yet, they do love you. Their lens is shaped by their fears and experiences, not by a desire to control or harm you. Recognizing this allows you to hold two truths at once: that they care deeply, and that your story is yours to live.

You are allowed to carve your own path, make choices that surprise them, and explore your identity without apology. Every time you take a step toward what feels true for you — whether that's picking a club that excites you, making new friends, pursuing a creative dream, or simply speaking up when you feel unheard — you are practicing courage, resilience, and authenticity. And every time your parents question, worry, or struggle to understand, it's not a failure on your part; it's just part of the process of growing up in a family where love, expectations, and individuality coexist.

Sometimes, your growth will create friction, and that's okay. Sometimes they'll say things that sting, or make rules that feel unfair, or fail to notice the little victories you achieve. But that doesn't make you wrong or ungrateful. You can honor their love while also honoring yourself. You can be patient with their fears while being bold with your dreams. You can hold compassion for the limitations of their understanding while expanding the horizon of your own. Your journey doesn't erase theirs; it adds a new layer to the family story, a continuation of something that started long before you were born.

And here's the best part: in navigating this space, you learn something beautiful about love, independence, and identity. You discover that love isn't always about agreement, that freedom isn't always about rebellion, and that understanding doesn't always arrive on your schedule. You learn to trust your instincts, to speak your truth, and to nurture your inner life with or without constant approval. And every small step you take — every choice to express yourself authentically, every time you advocate for your needs, every time you show up as yourself even when it's uncomfortable — is an act of bravery. It's a declaration that you are allowed to grow, to change, and to shine in ways that might be unfamiliar to them.

So, even when your parents don't fully get it, even when love sounds like fear and freedom sounds like rebellion, remember this: you are not alone, you are not wrong, and your journey is worthy. You are allowed to be the main character of your own story, and part of growing up is learning how to hold love for others while holding space for yourself. Every choice to speak, explore, and claim your life — even when it's messy, misunderstood, or scary — is a testament to your strength, your courage, and your humanity. That is brave. That is growth. That is real life.

"Sometimes love sounds like fear, and freedom sounds like rebellion. But truthfully? You're just growing up — and that's brave."

Advice from Me to You

• **Talk to them like they're scared, not evil.** Remember, most of the time, your parents aren't trying to frustrate or control you on purpose — they're scared. Scared of what might happen to you, scared of mistakes, scared of letting go of the "rules" they grew up with. So, when you feel misunderstood or pushed around, try to approach them with empathy. Instead of reacting with anger or rolling your eyes, imagine having a conversation with someone who is worried, even if it feels irrational. Sometimes just acknowledging their fear — without giving up your own voice — softens tension and makes dialogue possible.

• **Let your actions speak louder than words.** You don't always need to argue to be understood. Show them who you are through consistency. Keep pursuing your passions, showing up to responsibilities, and living in a way that reflects your values. When they see you being steady, responsible, and thoughtful, their trust in your independence grows naturally. Over time, actions often speak louder than lectures or debates, and your parents will begin to see the real you — not just the version filtered through worry or assumptions.

• **Don't shrink**. You are not a smaller version of your parents, and your life doesn't have to fit inside the box they imagine. Your dreams, thoughts, emotions, and quirks are all valid. Claim your space physically, mentally, and emotionally. Speak up for your choices. Dress, speak, and live in a way that feels authentic to you. Shrinking might feel like the easier path in the moment, but it won't help anyone — not you, not them, not your relationship. Standing tall and showing your individuality is not rebellion; it's self-respect.

• **Build your support circle.** You don't have to navigate this journey alone. Find people who get you — friends, cousins, mentors, teachers, or even online communities — who understand your perspective, validate your feelings, and cheer for your growth. Having people outside the family who see and appreciate the real you can make it easier to stay confident and balanced. They act as mirrors, reminding you that your value doesn't depend on anyone's misunderstanding or disagreement.

• **Give them grace** — and give yourself freedom. This is the hardest but most important part. Your parents are learning, just like you are. They may not always get it right, just as you won't always navigate your own life perfectly. Giving them grace means understanding that they love you in their own imperfect way. Giving yourself freedom means honoring your own needs, choices, and identity without guilt or apology. And here's the magical part: both can exist at the same time.

You can love and respect your parents while still claiming your independence. You can hold compassion for their fears and expectations while also trusting your instincts. You can create a life that is uniquely yours, without feeling like you have to erase them or yourself in the process.

Chapter 12

Not Everyone Likes You (And That's Okay)

Because being universally liked isn't the goal — being real is.

The Story: "The Girl Who Just Didn't Like Me"

Let's rewind to when I was 15.

There was this one girl in school — let's call her Tanya. Tanya had a loud laugh, a polished group of friends, and this habit of shooting me that look whenever I raised my hand in class. You know the look — half amusement, half judgment, like my very existence was an inside joke she wasn't letting me in on.

The thing is... I hadn't done anything to her. I wasn't part of her circle, I never spread gossip, and we barely interacted. But still, it was obvious: Tanya didn't like me.

And the worst part? That fact completely hijacked my brain.

I'd sit at my desk, staring at my notebook, wondering what invisible mistake I'd made. I'd replay every conversation I'd had that week, scroll through my own Instagram captions, and overanalyze every laugh at lunch.

Was I being too much? Too quiet? Too confident? Too awkward?

Basically, I turned into a one-woman overthinking machine.

And soon, it wasn't just about Tanya. I began assuming other people secretly felt the same. I edited myself like I was editing a photo: I cropped out the messy parts, lowered the volume on my laugh, and toned down my opinions. Every room I walked into felt like a stage, and I watched faces like they were live reaction buttons.

But then, one random evening while doom-scrolling through Pinterest, I saw a quote that stopped me in my tracks:

"You could be the ripest, juiciest peach in the world, and there will still be someone who hates peaches."

And something clicked.

Maybe Tanya didn't need a reason not to like me. Maybe it wasn't about me at all — it was about her taste, her triggers, her perceptions. Maybe she saw something in me that unsettled her, or reminded her of something she couldn't stand in herself. Or maybe — and this was the most freeing thought of all — maybe she just didn't vibe with me. And that was okay. That was so okay.

Because here's the truth: in a world where being "liked" feels like social currency, you don't actually need to be everyone's favorite flavor. Your people — the ones who really see you — they'll get it. And the rest? They'll just scroll past.

The Real Talk

Here's the hard truth that no one really tells you: not everyone is going to like you. And honestly? That's not just okay — it's normal.

Think about it. Even the most loved people in the world have critics. There are bestselling authors with one-star reviews. Grammy-winning artists with people who hate their songs. Even your favorite actor or creator has a comment section full of both love and shade. So why would you be any different?

When you decide to be yourself — fully, unapologetically, loudly, or softly — you're going to stand out. And standing out makes some people uncomfortable. Some won't get you. Some will misjudge you. Some may even project their insecurities onto you. But none of that is your job

to fix.
What people think of you says more about them than it does about you. Their likes and dislikes are shaped by their own stories, insecurities, and moods. You can be the kindest, most thoughtful version of yourself, and still, someone will roll their eyes. And that doesn't cancel your kindness — it just shows where they are at.
When you bend and shrink yourself just to be "liked," you lose the very magic that makes you - you. Imagine watering down vibrant paint until it's just grey — safe, invisible, forgettable. That's what happens when you edit yourself to please everyone.
So, let's flip the perspective: being disliked isn't proof that you're doing something wrong. Sometimes, it's proof that you're living your truth. Your boldness, your laughter, your quiet confidence, your honesty — they'll never be everyone's cup of tea. And that's a good thing. You're not here to be tea. You're here to be you.

Life Lesson + Big Sister Advice

Here's what I need you to remember:

• **You are not a mirror**. You're not here to reflect what others want to see. If someone labels you "too much" or "not enough," that's just a reflection of their expectations, not your reality.

• **Being liked is not the finish line**. If you spend your whole life chasing approval, you'll keep running in circles — because what one person applauds, another person criticizes. You can't win that game, and you're not supposed to.
• **Your real people will find you**. The ones who laugh at your weird jokes, who don't flinch when you speak your mind, who see your heart without needing explanations — those are the ones worth holding close. You don't have to audition for them.
• **Be proud of your own company**. You are the one person you'll spend every single day of your life with. So, the most important approval you'll ever earn is your own. When you're real with yourself — honest about your flaws, proud of your strengths, gentle with your growth — you won't feel desperate for anyone else's validation.

And here's **the golden rule: your worth is not up for debate**. It doesn't rise when someone claps for you, and it doesn't fall when someone gossips about you. It just is. Solid. Steady. Untouchable.

So next time someone doesn't like you, instead of spiraling, shrug and say:

"I'm not Wi-Fi, babe. I don't need to connect with everyone."

Chapter 13

Main Character Energy

Let's set the scene.

You're walking down the street, headphones in, your playlist blasting. Not just any playlist—the one you've curated for vibes only. The one where every track feels like it was made to soundtrack your life. The bass drops exactly when your sneakers hit the pavement, and the chorus comes in right as you turn the corner. Suddenly, you're not just walking—you're strutting, like the pavement itself rolled out as your personal red carpet.

The sunlight catches your hair at that perfect angle, making you glow like some Instagram filter you didn't even apply. The breeze tugs at your shirt, just enough to give you that accidental "music video" look. Cars honk, people shuffle past, but you're not focused on any of them. For once, the noise of the world fades into the background.

In that moment, it feels like time has slowed. You catch your reflection in a shop window, and for a split second, you don't just see yourself. You see the **star of the story.** The version of you who always existed, but you never paused long enough to notice and maybe nobody else notices it. To them, you're just another person walking down the street, ear buds in, minding your business. But to you? It feels like a scene. The camera is on you. The light is on you. The story is on you.

That's your **Main Character Moment.**

And here's the best part: you don't need a film crew, dramatic lighting, or Hollywood special effects to make it real. You don't need to be in New York, sipping overpriced coffee with a trench coat flying behind you. You don't need to wait for a perfect skin day, the dream friend group, or your *"glow-up era"* to begin.

You just need you.

Because you always were—and always will be—**the author, the narrator, the director, and the lead role in your own life**. Nobody else gets to write your plot. Nobody else gets to decide when your big moment happens. Nobody else gets to play your role, because they don't have your script.

But here's where it gets tricky.
We forget this. All the time.
We get caught up in **side roles:**

• Being the helper, the supporter, the quiet one in the background.
• Comparing ourselves to the "cooler," "prettier," "smarter" characters we see around us.
• Editing our own sparkle down, as if it'll make other people more comfortable.

And somewhere in the middle of people-pleasing, shrinking ourselves, and scrolling through everyone else's highlight reels, we start believing we're just an extra. A background character in someone else's movie.
But that's the lie.

The truth? Sometimes your story is soft and slow. Sometimes it's chaotic and messy. Sometimes it feels like nothing is happening at all, and sometimes it feels like everything is happening all at once. But no matter what, your story is worth telling.

Main Character Energy isn't about perfection. It's about presence.

It's not about always being glamorous, flawless, or "aesthetic." It's about realizing that *this moment*—the ordinary, everyday moment you're in right now—is just as worthy of attention as the big, shiny milestones.

Main Character Energy is sipping coffee like it's a scene in a French indie film. It's tying your shoelaces before leaving the house like it's the calm before your big action sequence. It's crying on your bed at 2 a.m. and realizing—yep, even this belongs in the movie. Because the main character doesn't disappear when things get messy. The main character owns every scene, the good and the bad.

And so do you.

So, remember this:

You don't need permission to shine. You don't need applause to validate your role. And you definitely don't need to wait for the "perfect moment."

Because the perfect moment? It's already here. The second you decide to notice it.

The Problem: Forgetting You're the Star

"Main Character Energy." Sounds cute, right? It's all over TikTok, Instagram Reels, and Pinterest boards. Aesthetic montages of people sipping matcha in Paris cafés, journaling with candles lit, twirling in flowy dresses under fairy lights. The captions scream: **romanticize your life!!**

And sure, those clips are fun. But what happens when your "main character's life" doesn't look like that?

Because real life?

Sometimes it looks like rushing out of the house with tangled hair and mismatched socks because you overslept—again.
Sometimes it looks like eating Maggi straight from the pot while Netflix asks, *"Are you still watching?"* (Yes, Netflix, I am. Stop judging me.)
Sometimes it looks like sitting in your room at 11:47 p.m., scrolling endlessly, watching other people's highlight reels, wondering, *Do I even have a storyline? Or am I just... filler content?*

Social Media & The "Extra" Feeling

Here's the trap: social media makes us feel like everyone else is the main character.

• One friend is always travelling to dreamy places, uploading sunset pictures with poetic captions.
• Another is posting gym selfies with motivational quotes, looking like they were born in a Nike ad.
• That one couple keeps dropping mushy "relationship goals" posts while you're just... third-wheeling through their stories.

• And then there's the random person you barely know who somehow went viral for eating noodles in slow motion.
Meanwhile, you're on the couch, still in yesterday's hoodie, debating whether or not to finally wash your hair.

And suddenly, you're not the star anymore. You're not even a named character. You're "background extra #27." The one walking past in the blurry part of the scene, while the real characters kiss, win trophies, or make life-changing announcements.

The Voice in Your Head

That "extra" feeling? That's not reality—it's your inner critic running commentary.

The voice says things like:

• "You're not doing enough."
• "Look at them—they're prettier, cooler, smarter, more successful."
• "You're too late. Everyone else is already ahead."
• "You don't matter as much as you think you do."

And the worst part? You believe it. You start to shrink. You clap for other people's wins but never celebrate your own. You edit yourself down, like you're trying not to take up too much space in your own story.

It's like you've accidentally accepted a role you never auditioned for: the *sidekick.* The background character. The supportive friend who boosts everyone else's glow-up but never gets their own.

Why We Shrink
We forget we're the star because life doesn't always feel cinematic.

- No background music swells when we're having a good day.
- No director yells "Cut!" when things get awkward.
- No audience claps when we finish a small task that actually felt huge.

So, we start telling ourselves that nothing we're doing is big enough to count. We convince ourselves that until we get the perfect grades, the dream job, the glow-up, the love story, we're just in the background.

But here's the thing: that's not true.

The Plot Twist

Being the main character isn't about being flawless, popular, or perfectly aesthetic.

It's not about the look of your life. It's about the *feel* of it.
It's about being **present.**
It's about choosing yourself—even when it's hard.
It's about realizing that the tiny, ordinary, quiet parts of your life are just as cinematic as the loud, flashy ones.

Main Character Energy isn't about proving yourself to the world. It's about reminding yourself that you've been the star all along.

So, the real problem isn't that you're not the main character. The real problem is that you keep forgetting you already are.

A Story: Not the Star… Yet

In school, I wasn't the star, not even close—I was the "supportive friend," the one who everyone could count on to clap the loudest during performances, to hold their bags during dance practice, to rehearse lines with them before a play, to take fifty photos until we found *the one* with the right lighting and angle. My gallery was full of their best moments; my camera rolls a museum of everyone else's glow. I was the walking, talking hype squad—the person who would scream "yes's queen!" across the hallway just to make someone's day. But when it came to me? I stayed small. If someone complimented me, I'd wave it off like it was a mistake. If there was a chance to shine, I'd step back before anyone could notice me. My whole identity became being the one who helped *others sparkle*, while convincing myself that maybe I wasn't meant to shine at all. And I told myself it was fine—after all, every movie has background characters, right? Maybe that was just my role.

Then came the day everything shifted, and funny enough, it wasn't even during some big dramatic moment. It was in class, on a random Tuesday afternoon. My favorite teacher had just finished giving back papers. I was sitting there, invisible as usual, trying to blend into the background, when she suddenly looked straight at me. With this mix of kindness and firmness, she asked, "Why are you hiding in the background of your own life?" And wow. That hit me harder than any grade or scolding ever had. I remember feeling frozen, like the entire classroom faded into slow motion, like in those movie scenes where the music cuts out, and the camera zooms in on the main character having their big realization. That one sentence cracked something inside me wide open.

I went home replaying her words over and over. And for the first time, I really saw myself—I saw the way I always shoved myself to the edges of group photos, the way I never volunteered for anything that put me in the spotlight, the way I poured endless energy into making others feel important but treated my own worth like an afterthought. I realized I had been so busy being the cheerleader, the helper, the sidekick, that I forgot I was allowed to be the main character too.

Of course, I didn't transform overnight. There was no magical glow-up montage. But I started small—whisper-small at first. I started saying yes to things I'd usually avoid: presenting in class, auditioning for the school play, and wearing that outfit I'd always wanted to but was too scared to pull off. I swapped "safe" hoodies for clothes that actually made me feel alive, not just hidden. I began walking into rooms like I belonged there, even if I didn't fully believe it yet. And little by little, something shifted. The world didn't collapse. My friends didn't abandon me. No one rolled their eyes when I took up space—in fact, some of them started cheering me on in the same way I used to cheer for them. Slowly, I stopped watching my life like an audience member and started living it like a star on stage.

That's when I realized: all those years, it wasn't that I didn't have a story worth telling. It was that I kept leaving myself out of it.

The Lesson: Your Life ≠ Side Character Arc

Here's the truth: *Main Character Energy* isn't about being the loudest person in the room or the prettiest, most fashionable, most productive one in the crowd. It isn't about having your life together 24/7, walking in with a slow-motion hair flip, or being the kind of person who has a carefully curated Instagram feed where every coffee cup looks like it belongs in Vogue. That's the surface-level version people try to sell online. The real thing goes much deeper.

Real Main Character Energy is about authenticity. It's about waking up and deciding, "I'm allowed to live my life in a way that feels real to me, not just the way that looks impressive to other people." It's about owning your weirdness, your quirks, your insecurities, your passions. It's about remembering that being important doesn't require a stage or a spotlight—it just requires presence.

The problem is, so many of us confuse being "main character" with being "perfect." We think we'll only get to be the star once we finally fix ourselves: once we lose the weight, once we get the glow-up, once we're in a relationship, once we have the right job, once we finally achieve something big enough to be clapped for. Until then, we shrink into side roles, convincing ourselves we're the background character in everyone else's stories. But here's the twist—your life isn't on pause until you become "perfect." It's happening right now. And you don't need to look or be a certain way for it to matter.

Think of it this way: if your life were a movie, you wouldn't only count the shiny parts as "real scenes." You wouldn't skip past the quiet breakfasts, the crying sessions, the awkward silences, the nights where you stayed up too late rewatching the same comfort show for the hundredth time. Those are the parts that make the story worth watching. Nobody goes to the movies to only see the climax; we care about the buildup, the rawness, the messy bits, because that's what makes the payoff feel real. Your life works the same way. The moments you keep dismissing as "boring" or "insignificant" are actually the golden threads that make your storyline richer.

Look at your daily life: the way the sunlight spills through your window in the morning, the way your playlist can flip your entire mood, the way a stranger holds the door open for you when you're carrying too many bags. Those are scenes. Micro-scenes, sure, but they're yours. And when you start noticing them, when you start treating them as part of the movie instead of throwaway footage, you start to realize just how much beauty is already woven into your ordinary days.

And yes—let's talk about the breakdowns too. The nights where you're curled up crying into your pillow, the mornings where you drag yourself out of bed even though everything in you wants to give up, the days where you feel like you're falling behind while the world races ahead. Those aren't failures. They're dramatic plot twists. They're the tension in your arc, the parts of the story that lead to growth, strength, and transformation. Every main character has those moments—the heartbreak, the betrayal, the rejection, the day everything feels like it's falling apart. In movies, we call them "character development." In life, we call them "hard days." But they serve the same purpose: they shape you into someone stronger, wiser, and more ready for the next chapter.

Here's the dangerous trap, though: when you forget you're the star of your own life, you start waiting. Waiting to be noticed. Waiting for someone to choose you. Waiting for your "big break." You hand over the pen and let everyone else write your script. You treat yourself like an extra—always clapping for other people's wins but never pausing to celebrate your own. You sit on the sidelines, hoping someone will pull you into the spotlight. But that's not how it works. Nobody else gets to write your story for you. Nobody else can live your life. The truth is harsh but freeing: if you don't step into your own role, the story doesn't get told the way it's meant to.

So, what does it actually mean to live like the main character? It means choosing yourself—actively, intentionally, every single day. It means giving yourself the same love and applause you so freely give others. It means recognizing that your life isn't a side character arc, it's the central storyline. You don't need to be the loudest, the prettiest, or the most successful to own that. You just need to start *believing it.*

Imagine treating the little things as sacred: your morning coffee as a ritual that sets the tone for the day. Your walk to school or work is a montage, headphones in, the world blurring around you.

Your late-night journaling is the script-writing part of your journey. Even your quiet dinners alone as the intimate, indie film moments. The more you romanticize those small things, the more you step into your narrative with pride.

And here's the kicker—when you start doing this, you stop needing

someone else to validate you. You stop waiting for someone to pick you for the team, or to notice you, or to tell you that you matter. You realize you were never auditioning in the first place. You've already had the lead role from the start. You just forgot to step onto the stage.

So let me remind you: your life is not a side plot. You're not a blurry extra in the background of someone else's love story or success montage. You are the main character, and this—right now, today, in all its messy, imperfect glory—is your scene.

Advice: How to Live Your Main Character Era

Romanticize Little Things

Not every main character moment looks like Paris at sunset—sometimes it looks like making Maggi at 2 a.m. with your playlist blasting and

Pretending you're in a cooking show. Light that random scented candle you bought three months ago "for later." Drink your chai or coffee in your favorite mug like it's a magical potion fuelling your whole plot. Take a boring bus ride and stare dramatically out the window like you're in a music video. Record a five-second clip of the rain like it's the opening shot of your documentary. Look at the moon and act like it's your personal director. The trick? Pretend even the tiniest things are cinematic—because when you treat your life like a movie, it starts feeling like one.

Rewrite Your Narrative

Your self-talk is literally the background narration of your story. Imagine if a Netflix show opened with a voiceover that said: *"Ugh, here's this awkward loser again."* You'd turn it off, right? So why are you saying that to yourself? Instead of *"I'm so cringe,"* try *"I'm still loading... like Wi-Fi."* Instead of *"I never get it right,"* try *"Main character in training arc."* Instead *of "Nobody notices me,"* try *"Plot twist: they will."* Life feels different when you start speaking about yourself like you're rooting for you. Narrate your own hype. Call yourself the protagonist out loud if you need to. Cheesy? Maybe. Effective? Absolutely.

Let Go Of Extra Auditions

Here's the tea: not every crowd deserves your sparkle. You don't need to keep auditioning for roles in someone else's story when your own script is waiting. If you're in a group where you're always quiet, always shrinking, always trying to prove you're enough—it's not your stage. Some people will never clap for you, and that's okay, because main characters don't chase approval; they build their own audience. Your people are the ones who laugh with you until your stomach hurts, who hype up the random Instagram story of your dog, who don't make you feel like you need subtitles for your personality. Stop fighting for side roles in someone else's movie—you've got your own to film.

Show Up for Yourself

Wear the outfit you've been "saving" for someday. Do the eyeliner even if you're just buying bread. Put on lip gloss for no one but yourself. Take yourself out on solo dates—a movie, a bookstore, even just sipping cold coffee in a café while scrolling Pinterest. Yeah, it feels weird at first, but then it feels like freedom. Speak your truth—even if your voice cracks like a bad Bluetooth speaker. Say "no" without guilt. Set boundaries without apologizing. The real glow-up is not about better skin or cooler shoes—it's about the way you show up for yourself. Treat yourself like you're worth it, because the truth is, you've always been.

Take Control of Plot

Main character arcs are never straight lines—they're full of messy rewrites, filler episodes, and sudden cliffhangers. Failed a test? Plot twist. Had a breakup? Character development. Moved schools? New season. Your story isn't ruined just because a chapter didn't go the way you planned—it just means the genre is shifting. You get to pick when a new arc starts. You get to say, *"This part doesn't fit anymore—I'm editing it out."* And you get to surprise everyone (including yourself) with a glow-up arc when they least expect it. Remember: main characters don't wait for permission to change the story—they grab the pen and rewrite.

So yeah, whether you're sipping chai on your balcony, binging K-dramas in pyjamas, or crying to a sad playlist at midnight—remember, the camera's still rolling. You're not a background character. You're the lead, and the world is lucky to be watching.

"The main character isn't a role, it's a mindset. Your life is the plot twist."

Chapter 14

The Mirror Lies Sometimes

Let's be real — we've all had those days where one look in the mirror ruins everything. You woke up feeling okay, maybe even kind of cute... until your reflection decided to go rogue. Suddenly, your skin looks off, your body looks "wrong," your hair feels like it belongs to another planet, and your brain whispers lies like, *"Why can't I look like her?"* or *"Nothing about me is enough."*

And it's wild, isn't it? Just one glance at your reflection can flip your entire mood. You could've been vibing, feeling calm, maybe even proud of yourself for showing up today, but then—boom—the mirror whispers, and suddenly you're spiraling. It's like this sneaky villain that waits until you're already vulnerable and then attacks.

But here's the truth most mirrors will never tell you: **your reflection isn't reality.** What you see in the mirror is filtered through your mood, your insecurities, your lack of sleep, and society's impossible beauty standards. The mirror doesn't show your laughter that makes people around you light up. It doesn't reflect your kindness, your resilience, the fire in your ideas, or the comfort of your presence. It doesn't show your courage when you stand up for a friend, or the way you make someone else feel seen just by listening. The mirror is just glass. Nothing more. It's not a measure of your worth, your beauty, or your place in this world.

The Real Enemy? Comparison.

The truth is, the mirror usually feels the harshest when we're already in a comparison spiral. Maybe you were scrolling through Instagram or TikTok, and suddenly, your brain got ambushed by flawless faces, dreamy bodies, *"perfect"* hair, and people who look like they woke up in an aesthetic morning routine ad. You put your phone down, glance in the mirror, and your brain instantly goes: *"Yeah... you don't measure up."*

But here's what's ironic — those perfect pictures aren't real either. They're crafted, edited, lit just right, filtered, posed, and retaken fifty times until they nailed "effortless." Even if they don't wake up looking like that. Even they have days when their mirror lies to them.

Comparison is the toxic friend that sneaks into your mind and convinces you that everyone else is winning, while you're somehow failing. And the mirror? It becomes the weapon that feeds the comparison monster, amplifying insecurities until they're louder than your inner cheerleader. And honestly? It's exhausting living like that.

A Mirror Story You Might Know

Take Riya, for example.

Riya used to avoid mirrors. Not because she didn't care about her appearance—actually, the opposite. She cared too much. Every time she walked past a reflective surface, it felt like a pop quiz she wasn't ready for.

On the outside, Riya looked like the kind of girl who had it all together. She dressed well, had good grades, and posted occasional selfies with her friends. But inside, it was a completely different story.

One morning stood out the most. She had a big presentation at school — the kind she'd been preparing for days. She'd stayed up late practicing, memorizing, making slides, but also overthinking every possible outcome. The pressure was already heavy.

That morning, as she stood in front of the mirror brushing her hair, the whispers started:

"Your face looks bloated."

"Why are your eyes so puffy?"

"You look tired. They'll notice."

"You don't look like someone who belongs at the front of the room."

She changed outfits. Once, twice, five times. Nothing worked. Nothing felt right. It was like the mirror had become a megaphone for her inner critic, shouting every insecurity back at her.

By the time she left home, she was drained. She skipped breakfast. She sat in the bathroom stall at school, crying quietly. She nearly backed out of the presentation, not because she wasn't prepared, but because she was convinced that she didn't "look" like someone capable of delivering it.

But when she finally got up to present? She crushed it. Her classmates clapped. Her teacher smiled proudly. A few students even came up to her afterwards, telling her how confident and inspiring she seemed.

That moment cracked something open for her. She realized: the mirror had lied. It hadn't reflected her hard work. It hadn't shown her courage or her voice or the way she commanded the room. It only reflected her fears that morning—and nothing else.

From then on, she didn't magically stop having bad mirror days. But something shifted. Whenever she caught herself spiraling in front of the glass, she started asking, *"Maybe it's not me. Maybe it's my mood talking."* And on those days, instead of trying to fight her reflection, she'd take a breath and remind herself: *"The mirror doesn't get the final word on who I am."*

Flip the Mirror: What if You're Not the Problem?

Here's the question nobody tells you to ask: what if your reflection isn't the enemy... what if the rules you've been taught about beauty are?

Think about it:

Who decided that acne is ugly?

Who decided that certain body types are "ideal"?

Who decided that tired eyes or textured skin means you're less worthy?

Was it an ad trying to sell you skincare? A toxic friend who made comments about your looks? A filtered influencer who doesn't even look like themselves in real life? Or was it years of silent conditioning from movies, magazines, and social media telling you what's "beautiful" and what's not?

Because the truth is, you don't need to shrink yourself to be loved. You don't need to hide to be accepted. You don't need validation from a rectangle on your wall or a perfectly edited selfie.

Instead of asking, *"What's wrong with me?"* flip it. Ask, *"Who told me this was wrong in the first place?"*

Some Days You Glow, Some Days You Grow

Not every day is a glow-up day. And honestly? That's okay. There will be days where your reflection and your feelings don't align. Days where your confidence is a little wobbly. Days when the mirror feels louder than your inner voice. But those are growth days.

Growth days are the ones that teach you to root your self-worth in things beyond your reflection. They teach patience, compassion, and perspective. They remind you that you're not just a face or a body—you're a full human being with layers, stories, and a future too big to be defined by today's insecurities.

Think about it: you've survived every bad mirror day so far. And you'll survive the next one too. Because your worth was never built on a reflection—it was built on your resilience.

So, when the mirror lies (and it will, sometimes), don't let it be the only voice you hear. Step back. Remember Riya's story. Remember your own story. Remember that you are always, always more than what you see.

Final Note:

You're not just a face. You're not just a body. You're not just a reflection. You're a soul, a mind, a work in progress. And progress—even when it's messy, even when it feels slow—is always beautiful.

"Your reflection can't capture your energy. Stop letting it define your entire vibe."

Chapter 15

Self-Love vs. External Validation

"If you live for their approval, you'll die by their rejection."

Let's Get Real

Let's be honest — compliments hit different. Someone says, *"Wow, you look so good today,"* and suddenly you're glowing brighter than a Diwali light string. Does your crush notice your new haircut? Boom, instant serotonin. You post a photo, and the likes roll in? Your phone basically becomes a slot machine of happiness.

But here's the plot twist: what happens when that doesn't happen?
When does the photo flop? When your crush doesn't notice? When nobody comments *"slay queen"?*
Do you suddenly feel smaller? Do you reread your own caption, wondering if it was cringe? Do you start asking, *"Wait, am I not enough?"*

That right there is the difference between **self-love and external validation.**

External validation is like fast food: quick, tasty, addictive — but ultimately leaves you bloated and unsatisfied.

Self-love? That's the home-cooked meal. Slow, nourishing, grounding. The kind that fills you up from the inside.

Why External Validation Feels So Addictive

Here's a fun (and slightly evil) fact: every time you get a like, compliment, or approval, your brain releases dopamine — the same "feel good" chemical you get from sugar, Netflix binges, or, let's be real, scrolling memes at 2 a.m. That's why it feels so good.

But there's a catch. Dopamine doesn't last long. It fades quickly, leaving you craving more. So, what do we do? We post again, dress up again, try harder again — hoping for another hit.

And social media knows this. It's literally designed to keep us hooked. The scrolling, the double-taps, the streaks — all engineered to keep us chasing validation like a hamster chasing snacks.

The problem is, when you rely only on outside approval, you hand over the keys to your happiness. Suddenly, your confidence is not in your hands — it's in the hands of strangers, classmates, even people you don't even like. And that's a dangerous place to live.

The Outfit That Changed Nothing (But Everything)

There was one day in 11th grade that I'll never forget. On the surface, nothing tragic happened. No dramatic betrayal. No school scandal. Just a Friday. But to me, it was a turning point.

Our school had this rare "no-uniform Friday." Sounds innocent, right? Finally, a chance to ditch the stiff blue salwar-kameez (or polo and pants) and actually dress how we wanted. But trust me, it was less "casual Friday" and more "Project Runway." People planned for days, curated Pinterest boards, begged older siblings for clothes, and even borrowed shoes.

And me? I fell straight into the spiral. I wanted to look perfect. Not just nice. Not just "you tried." Perfect. Cool. Hot. Effortless. All at once. (Spoiler: that's not possible.)

So, I copied a creator I was obsessed with at the time: cropped lavender top, layered silver chains, ripped high-waist jeans, winged eyeliner (a risk, because let's be real — eyeliner is a gamble), and a sleek bun that fought against every curl on my head.

Was I comfortable? Absolutely not. But I convinced myself the outfit would do the heavy lifting. I wanted reactions. Whispers. Double takes. And, if I'm brutally honest, I wanted him — the boy from my chemistry class — to notice.

And at first, it worked. Heads turned when I walked in. A couple of girls complimented me. Someone whispered, "She looks different today." That dopamine hit? Fireworks. I floated through the first hour.

But then the cracks showed.

- The crop top wouldn't stay in place, so I kept tugging it down as my life depended on it.
- I ran to the bathroom between classes to fix my eyeliner that kept smudging.
- I laughed too hard at jokes that weren't funny, desperate to seem confident.
- I barely ate lunch because I was scared my stomach would show.
- And all day long, I waited. For him. For that one comment. That one look.

It never came. By the last class, I wasn't floating anymore. I was exhausted. Not physically, but emotionally. I felt like I had performed all day, like

I was auditioning for a role in a play I didn't even like.
That evening, I stood in front of my mirror, makeup half-melted, hair escaping its bun, and asked myself something I had never asked before: "Did I even like how I looked today?"
The answer was no. I liked that others liked it. That's different.
And that realization cracked me open.

The Rebuild

The following week, I tried something new. Nothing dramatic. Just... me. Regular uniform day. Hair tied in a messy half-bun like I usually do at home. Quirky earrings I loved but was scared to wear. No makeup.

And guess what? A few people still said, *"You look cute today."* But here's the twist — this time, I believed it. Because I had already told myself.

From that day, I started rebuilding. Slowly.

- Wearing colors that made *me* happy, not just ones that are trending on Instagram.
- Posting reels that made me laugh, even if no one else cared.
- Saying no to "cool" plans that drained me.
- Complimenting myself before waiting for anyone else to.

It wasn't perfect. I still sometimes catch myself checking likes too often, or waiting for someone to say something nice. But I also realized something bigger:

"self-love isn't loud. It's quiet. It's steady. And it doesn't disappear when the crowd goes silent."

Self-Love vs. External Validation: The Real Difference

We confuse these two all the time. Let's break it down:

- **External Validation** is loud, addictive, and quick. It thrives on applause, likes, and DMs. It feels amazing in the moment, but empties fast. It's like chasing confetti in the wind — fun, but impossible to hold.
- **Self-love** is quieter. It's how you talk to yourself after you fail. It's choosing rest without guilt. It's wearing the outfit you adore, even if nobody else gets it. It's rooting your worth in something no one else can touch.

The danger with external validation is this: it makes your confidence fragile. It rises when people notice you, and crashes when they don't. But self-love? That stays. Through bad skin days.

Through being left unseen. Through photos that flop.

It's the difference between building your home on quicksand vs. solid ground.

Final Note

Self-love is a practice, not a destination. You don't wake up one day and magically never care about validation again. You'll still want compliments sometimes. You'll still hope your post gets noticed. That's human. But the difference is, you won't depend on it for survival.

Because once you start choosing yourself — over and over again — the crowd becomes background noise. Nice, sure, but not necessary.

Or, as I like to say:

"I'd rather be whole alone than half-loved by the crowd."

www.ingramcontent.com/pod-product-compliance
Ingram Content Group UK Ltd.
Pitfield, Milton Keynes, MK11 3LW, UK
UKHW040037200726
13845UKWH00054B/424